Plane Crazy

Plane Crazy
A Celebration of Flying

Burton Bernstein

with illustrations by
Edward Koren

Ticknor & Fields · New York 1985

Library of Congress Cataloging in Publication Data

Bernstein, Burton.
Plane crazy.

"Most of the text of this book originally appeared
in The New Yorker."—T.p. verso.
1. Bernstein, Burton   2. Air pilots—United States—
Biography.   I. Title.
TL140.B45A36   1985   629.13'092'4 [B]   85-8155
ISBN 0-89919-390-0

Printed in the United States of America

P   10   9   8   7   6   5   4   3   2   1

Most of the text and drawings in this book originally appeared
in *The New Yorker*. The author thanks that magazine
for its permission to reprint the material herein.

FOR JANE,
sometime co-pilot
and full-time helpmeet

Foreword

IT is an oft-told tale, I admit. The yearning of the human being to fly like a bird in the sky has been told dozens of times, movingly and dreadfully, since the myth of Icarus. One could argue a good literary case that no more need be written on the subject since the works of Antoine de Saint-Exupéry, of a half century ago. Yet there is something about the continuing wonder of flight that makes writers of various stripes persevere — all of them trying to describe, poetize, articulate the strange longing.

Alas, I am no exception. From the time that I became a licensed airman (at age sixteen) and a writer-reporter (not long thereafter), I have wanted to combine the two noble disciplines for my own version of the theme. Like all pilots, I feel compelled to talk about flying. So, at long last, here is my story of one boy-man's love affair with aviation.

And it is also the story, through his idiomatic drawings, of one artist's fascination with flying and the people who fly. Although he's not a licensed pilot, Ed Koren has created drawings that bespeak a deep affection for the contagious preoccupation. I thank him for his good work and his company.

I thank, too, William Shawn, the editor of *The New Yorker*, for his indulgence and encouragement; C. Patrick Crow, Sara Lippincott, and Bill McKibben for their talents as *New Yorker* nonfiction editors; Candida Donadio and Eric Ashworth for their believing in this book as agents and friends; Katrina Kenison, my editor at Ticknor & Fields; the dedicatee for her service above and beyond; and, of course, all the people, mentioned and unmentioned in the book, who have helped by simply being the good people they are.

Plane Crazy

Sunday, March 28, 1948
Norwood, Massachusetts

ON this crisp morning, George R. Wiggin, a dour, weathered flight instructor, climbs out of the rattly yellow Piper J-3 Cub (N2123) that he and I have been flying together for the past fifteen minutes and tells me to take the tiny airplane up alone, to solo. His almost casual permission marks the culmination of ten hours of dual instruction, begun in August of 1946, when I was fourteen years old. "Remember not to dive at the runway when you're landing," he shouts above the sputter of the idling sixty-five-horsepower Continental engine. "If you're too high, slip the airplane in or go around again, but *don't dive!* I'll be standing right here watching. After you land, taxi back to the flight line and park the airplane. Good luck." He reaches into the cockpit, tightens the safety belt on the seat that he has just vacated, and adjusts the elevator-trim control to compensate for his absent weight. Then he closes the double-door hatch, slaps the doped fabric of the fuselage, which reverberates like a tomtom, and waves. I take a deep breath and embark on the greatest experience of my young life.

Actually, I have been adequately prepared to solo since last December, but I hadn't then turned sixteen, the legal minimum age for a student-pilot license. Mr. Wiggin became suspicious when he noticed that I always arrived at the Norwood Airport for my lessons by hitchhiking or, in one memorable instance, under the automotive auspices of my terrified mother. "You don't have a driver's license, do you?" he said to me one day. "You're not even sixteen yet."

I nodded sheepishly.

"How the hell do you expect to be a licensed student pilot if you're not even a licensed automobile driver? When you can drive to the airport all by yourself, I'll let you fly an airplane all by yourself." Today, for the first time, I legally drove to the airport, and Mr. Wiggin was as good as his word.

My eagerness to be the sole occupant and operator of an airplane long predated my flying lessons. At the age of five, I had become infatuated with aviation, having found myself within touching distance of a Stearman biplane parked at a small grass strip in southern Massachusetts. From then on, the mere sight, sound, or photograph of a plane sent volts of excitement through me. I drew childish pictures of aircraft on surfaces ranging from my bedroom wallpaper to school-textbook pages; I built balsa-wood-and-doped-paper models of Piper Cubs and P-47s; I read Antoine de Saint-Exupéry and how-an-airplane-flies books for children and opaque flight manuals for adult professionals; and I served as a junior airplane spotter for the Massachusetts State Guard during the Second World War and cursed my lot in not being old enough to become a fighter pilot. Later, I wheedled my parents into letting me take flying lessons, but had to use my allowance, school-lunch money, and odd-job wages to pay for them. My friends called me "plane crazy"; they couldn't figure out why I wasn't more interested in girls or sports or getting into a good college than in flying planes on weekends. But the sacrifices I made for Mr. Wiggin's time and his Piper Cubs were inconsequential. I reveled in the thrill of flying and his stern instruction in straight-and-level flight, climbs and glides, turns and slips, landings and takeoffs, recovery from spins and stalls, and — once, after a blizzard — operating a Cub equipped with aluminum skis. He corrected my mistakes with a stentorian "No!" and a wrenching of the controls to their proper setting; he approved my performance by remaining silent, and his silence was more gratifying than a pat on the back or a kind word.

On this momentous Sunday in March, he reviews the basic maneuvers during our fifteen minutes of dual flight and then decides to let me solo.

Fighting off a kind of giddiness, I apply myself to the serious matter at hand. If all goes well, I will perform a neat rectangle of controlled flight, causing this flimsy, ungainly machine to rise into the air above the east-west runway against a moderate easterly wind; to climb to six hundred feet and turn ninety degrees to the left for the crosswind leg of the closed traffic pattern; then to climb to eight hundred feet and make another ninety-degree left turn for the long downwind leg; and to make still another ninety-degree left turn for the base leg, followed by a shallow power-off glide, a turn to the final approach, and a safe landing on the same east-west runway. I ease the throttle forward a bit and taxi to the west end of the runway, where I brake to a full stop. So far so good. But suddenly everything I have learned about taking off crowds my mind in a numbing blur. For a panicky few moments, I have no idea what to do next except, perhaps, cut the engine and flee the airplane for terra firma. However, the sight of the carburetor-heat knob in the "on" position brings me back to my senses; the carburetor heater — which warms the carburetor to prevent the formation of ice — should be off for maximum power. I push the knob to the "off" position, release the brakes, line up on the runway, and open the throttle to full power. Without the weight of Mr. Wiggin in the tandem seat of the Cub, the plane gains flying speed at an alarming rate. It wants desperately to fly before I have rolled even two hundred feet along the runway. I move the control stick slightly forward to raise the tail, and, without any further effort on my part, the Cub springs into the air, climbing faster than it has ever climbed before. The airplane has simply taken itself off. I am almost an innocent passenger.

Soon, though, the little plane needs a pilot, and it astounds me to realize that I am the only pilot available. The wonder of this large fact inspires me, too. I diligently perform each step by rote, directing the obliging Cub to the downwind leg. Only then do I dare take a few seconds from my duties to look out the side window at the world eight hundred feet below — familiar countryside, buildings, and highways still in their winter drab but shining for me on this glorious day with grace and beauty. Indeed, U.S. Route 1 is the most beautiful thing I have ever seen. I am as one with Saint-Exupéry.

"OK, now land the plane," I tell myself. The carburetor-heated, power-off final approach to the runway goes without a hitch, but the irregular east wind seems to keep the plane flying longer than I want it to fly. I am over the runway's edge and still about two hundred feet above the ground. "Don't dive at the runway," I say for the absent Mr. Wiggin. "Just slip the airplane in a little." I slip the airplane in a little, and it banks crookedly to a stall just over the runway. I straighten it out with the rudder pedals and pull back the stick until it presses against my stomach. The Cub — still obliging, forgiving — hits the paved surface, bounces once, twice, and at last rolls slowly on its main landing gear and tiny tail wheel. I note with pride that there is still a lot of runway ahead of me as I brake and turn warily onto the taxiway. Not bad, I think. Not good, either. But I did it — I soloed!

Back at the flight line, I park the Cub and cut the engine. Mr. Wiggin is waiting there, not smiling. After I extricate myself from the plane, he shakes my hand. "It was OK," he says. "But you could have run out of runway." Later, he enters in my logbook "1st solo OK."

I continue to fly, both dual and solo, until February of 1949. I want nothing more than to fly, and be a professional aviator someday. But I run out of money, and, to tell the truth, other interests occupy me — girls, sports, getting into a good college. "You're finally growing up," my parents tell me, and my friends agree. At the beginning of my freshman year in college, after a classmate has died in a private-airplane crash, I stop thinking about flying.

Saturday, August 17, 1957

Spring Valley, New York

On this humid afternoon, George Morrin, another dour, weathered flight instructor, climbs out of the rattly yellow Aeronca 7AC Champ (N85700) that he and I have been flying together for the past fifty-five minutes and tells me to solo. Nine months ago, I was discharged from the Army and came to New York City to gain employment as a writer; soon, with a steady income and few responsibilities, I caught the flying bug again. The lure was enhanced when I discovered that as a veteran I could take flying lessons under the G.I. Bill of Rights, which would cover seventy-five per cent of the cost. The Spring Valley Airport, a small field in a heavily settled area of Rockland County alongside the New York State Thruway, was an easy bus ride from Manhattan, and the flight school there was inexpensive. Despite a short main runway that ran uphill from east to west — and gave the airport a dubious reputation among local pilots ("If you can land at Spring Valley, you can land anywhere," I often heard) — I liked the place. The atmosphere was relaxed, and the school's trainer, the Aeronca Champ, was a "taildragger," a close relative of the old Piper J-3 Cub. Like the Cub, the Champ was a stripped-down, basic airplane: no landing flaps, no radio, no navigational equipment beyond a magnetic compass, no frills — just a fabric-covered high-wing monoplane fitted out with only the most essential instruments, a reliable engine, and a forgiving nature. Relearning to fly was a piece of cake, to use a phrase pilots are fond of, and I was deemed ready to solo after five and a half hours' review of the fundamentals. Apart from the fun of flying again, what I liked most was the view from a few thousand feet over the Hudson River: the hazy city skyline, the gray elevations of West Point, and the magnificent river itself, which made visual navigation another piece of cake. On a hot summer day, for instance, one could fly south over the river to the Statue of Liberty, turn a hundred and eighty degrees around the statue, and head back to Spring Valley, marveling at the sights and breathing the cool, clean air rushing through the open side window. Commercial airliners occasionally made things a little dicey, especially when their wash caused spasms of turbulence, but that was all part of the game of modern aviation. A far more hazardous part of the game was the insane stunt of flying under the George Washington Bridge, which some daredevils performed from time to time, with mixed results. Whenever the adventures of one of these "flat-hatters" surfaced at the Quonset hut that served as the Spring Valley flight-school office, my instructor would say ruefully, "There are old pilots and there are bold pilots, but there are no old bold pilots."

At the time of my second "first" solo, I am a somewhat timorous pilot, but I have enough kid in me still to tingle over the event. I take off uphill to the west. In the humid, thin afternoon air, the plane struggles to leave the ground. Once airborne and over a housing development abutting the Thruway, I fly with a certain forced insouciance through the established traffic pattern, almost identical to the one at Norwood. After all, I have been a licensed student pilot, according to my logbook, for more than nine years. I take time to enjoy the view. But my final approach is too high for the strange, short runway, and I suddenly do not feel confident enough to attempt a steep sideslip. Embarrassed and perspiring, I push the throttle to full power and go around the pattern again, ultimately touching down on the first third of the runway — a good landing. "You did the right thing," Mr. Morrin says after I park the Champ. "If in doubt, don't — just go around again." And, as Mr. Wiggin had done, he writes in my logbook "1st solo OK." I have lived through another first solo, and while it is no longer the greatest experience of my life it comes precious close.

Weather and weekends permitting, I solo a great deal in the Aeronca Champ, flying extended routes that require visual pilotage and dead-reckoning navigation (they're known as "cross-country" flights) to Danbury, Connecticut; Poughkeepsie and Albany, New York; Morristown and Red Bank, New Jersey; and Great Barrington, Massachusetts. I am close to taking my examination for a private pilot's license (it would permit me to carry passengers) when my G.I. Bill money runs out along with my footloose bachelordom. Later, after my daughter is born, I put aside flying for the weighty responsibilities of fatherhood. Once again, relatives and friends tell me, "You're finally growing up." But I still get a funny feeling whenever I see a small plane flying overhead.

Friday, July 24, 1981
Danbury, Connecticut

THE morning, hot and clear, has the makings of a fine summer day. I wake up early, breakfast, and stroll across my back yard, in a small town north of Danbury, to my studio. But the day is too beautiful to sit in a studio writing. A small plane flies overhead, its aluminum skin glinting in the morning sun. I look up, as usual, and think, What a great day for flying! It's a thought that has struck me lately even on days not so great for flying. It has been more than twenty years since the last entry was inked in my logbook. Now I am middle-aged, with fewer responsibilities and more malaise. Maybe I should take up flying again — or, at least, find out what it would require these days to win back my license. Why the hell not? I give in to the whim, and twenty-five minutes later I'm parking my car in front of a flight school at the Danbury Municipal Airport.

There are three flight schools at the Danbury Airport, and I decide to make some inquiries at the first one I see — the Bluebird Aviation Corporation, housed in an appropriately blue prefabricated-steel shed, which serves as both office and hangar. Four Cessnas of various sizes are tied down on a grass apron outside the office door, and I feel a charge of excitement at just being close to these planes. A matronly woman is walking an apricot poodle among the parked airplanes. The dog spots me and barks ferociously. "It's all right, Zip," the woman says to the dog; then, to me, "He just doesn't like people wearing hats." I am wearing a red baseball cap, which I guess I put on because it somehow reminded me of my youthful flying days. After I explain to her that I was once a licensed pilot and would like some information about renewing my license, she says that her son, Richard King, is the owner of the Bluebird Aviation Corporation and can tell me what I want to know, once he returns to the office. We chat until he arrives. She is Harriett King, the widow of James Douglas King, who was the founder of Bluebird and who died in 1975 after a career in aviation dating back to the early nineteen-thirties. Until 1966, she says, the Kings leased and ran the airport at Armonk, New York — a small general-aviation field that was erased by the construction of Interstate 684 through Westchester County. The highway now courses along what used to be the airport's north-south runway, and a Ramada Inn stands where the operations building once was. "Highways and developments always seem to take over small airports sooner or later," Mrs. King says, with a light sigh. "I suppose they'll get us here at Danbury one day. The Danbury Fair Grounds, right next door, are going to be turned into a big, fancy shopping mall, I understand. People always want an airport in a city until they discover that the land is more profitable for stores or condominiums or something."

Her son — a tall, lean, black-haired man with regular features, a poster image of a mature pilot — arrives and invites me into the Bluebird office. I repeat my story, and he tells me that he does most of the charter flying, in Bluebird's twin-engine Piper Seneca, and that the flight instruction is conducted by David Smith, who should be along shortly. I find Richard King's manner typical of professional pilots I have known: friendly yet wary of strangers — even other pilots, until they prove their aviating abilities. I feel that I must impress him, so I show him my old logbook. He looks through the yellowing pages and allows himself a slight smile. "I know the Norwood Airport, and Spring Valley, too," he says. "I even remember old Mr. Wiggin at Norwood. I see that you once flew in to the Armonk Airport, which my dad used to run." Under the tutelage of his father, Richard learned to fly in Piper Cubs and Aeronca Champs, and this gives us something in common to talk about. "My father would sit in the rear seat," Richard says, "and he'd bop me on the back of my head when I did something wrong. Now, there was a tough pilot — and here comes another one."

Dave Smith enters the office, fresh from a session at the Connecticut Motor Vehicle Department, where he went to straighten out some registration problem with his car. In his midtwenties and full of the intensity of those years, Dave holds forth on the picayune regulations of bureaucracy. When Richard hands him my logbook to peruse, Dave chuckles, and says, "If I were in the Motor Vehicle Department, I'd say I can't look at your log because it's blue, or something like that." I notice that Dave affects more of a flier's style than Richard does — military aviator's sunglasses and shirt, for instance — but his young face works against the image. The subject of motor-vehicle regulations leads to the subject of federal aviation regulations and how they've changed flying in the past two decades. Danbury, they explain, is a controlled airport, with a tower manned by federal air-traffic controllers. Radio clearance is mandatory here, even while a pilot is taxiing. "It's not like the old days, when you just flew in or out of the traffic pattern as you liked, or you waited for a green light from the tower," Dave says. "Now you need permission for everything. Of course, the basic responsibility to see and avoid other aircraft still rests with the individual pilot, like before. You might suppose the government has taken all the fun out of flying, but I think you can still have a good time, in spite of the controls and regs. If you're still interested, why don't you go up with me for an hour in one of our Cessna trainers and see how you like it? Maybe you won't like how it's all changed since the Piper Cubs, and you won't want to continue." He pauses for me to consider his suggestion. I consider it for about ten seconds and agree to go up for an hour.

Dave directs me to N25042 — a brown-and-white Cessna 152 with two adjacent seats, a hundred-and-ten-horsepower Lycoming engine, landing flaps, and lights, and with various antennas protruding from its aluminum skin. It has trim, feminine lines, unlike the stubby, masculine Cub and Champ. Svelte as it is, the plane is nevertheless intimidating. Dave walks me through a detailed pre-flight inspection and orientation. He explains all the unfamiliar gadgets: the fuel sampler (for draining off a few ounces of hundred-octane low-lead gasoline from the tanks and carburetor to see if condensation or impurities are present), the VHF radio (for both communication and navigation), the emergency locater transmitter (designed to function automatically after a crash), the sturdy, steerable nose wheel (instead of the taildragger's tail wheel, which is what I'm used to), the control yoke (instead of a simple joystick), and an array of dials, circuit breakers, switches, levers, knobs, and buttons. He is a good, patient explainer.

We settle into the tight cockpit — I in the pilot's seat, Dave, to the right, in the co-pilot's, with its dual controls — and we buckle on our safety belts and harness straps. "Follow me as I go through the printed checklist here," Dave says. "You'll catch on quick. It's like riding a bike." Not quite. The engine starts with merely a turn of the ignition switch — nobody outside has to shout "Contact!" and spin the propeller, as with the Cub and the Champ. But most unfamiliar, and confusing, is the initial radio exchange between Dave and the controller in the concrete-steel-and-glass tower across the field. "Danbury ground, Cessna two-five-zero-four-two at Bluebird to active," Dave says matter-of-factly into the tubular microphone, and a rapid-fire response in squawking gibberish crackles from the overhead speaker. All I can glean from the answer is something about "two-six" and the words "wind" and "altimeter." Dave understands the gibberish perfectly and says in acknowledgment, "Zero-four-two" — the last three digits of the plane's identification number. He notices my bewildered look and says, "Don't worry about the radio stuff. I'll tell you about it later. Now we're going to taxi to the run-up area at the end of Runway Two-six. That's an east-west runway, the longest at Danbury. You know that the 'two-six' refers to two hundred and sixty degrees by the compass, so if you take off or land on Two-six you're heading into the west, against a westerly wind. If you take off or land from the other end of the runway, you're on Runway Eight, or heading eighty degrees by the compass — and going east. You remember all that from before, don't you?" I do, but it's good to be reminded. "Now let's see if you remember how to taxi."

I assume the controls and add power, and the Cessna moves. Steering the plane along the ground with the rudder pedals and, occasionally, the brake pedals comes back to me, and it is fun. We hold for our run-up at the end of Runway 26 (a run-up is the pre-takeoff testing of the engine at a high power setting), and then Dave radios the tower for clearance to take off. More gibberish. After what I gather is our clearance, we taxi to the runway's center line. "OK, let's go," Dave tells me. "Take off." With my left hand gripping the control wheel, I push the throttle in completely with my right hand, and the Cessna stirs into roaring motion. When we are about a third of the way down the long runway, the airspeed indicator registers fifty knots. "The airplane will fly now," Dave says calmly, and I ease the yoke back. The plane immediately leaves the ground, its nose pointed above the horizon. Before we reach two hundred feet of altitude, I know I'm hooked — plane crazy again.

We leave the traffic pattern, climb to twenty-five hundred feet, and turn northeast toward a practice area over a heavily wooded stretch of Roxbury, Connecticut. The fundamentals of flying magically come back to me as I bank, turn, and attempt straight-and-level flight, but my self-assurance is punctured by Dave's patter of criticism. I am piloting, yes, but not very well. But, my God, it's a wonderful sensation. Below us to the southeast is the Waterbury-Oxford Airport, and Dave suggests that we land there. "They got an old P-51 Mustang and an F8F Bearcat based at Oxford," he says. "Let's have a look at them." He must have guessed my affection for Second World War fighter planes. "I'll take it in. You keep your hands and feet lightly on the controls and follow me through." His approach and landing are effortless and flawless, the buzzer that signifies stall speed sounding just a second before we touch down. Following him through, I have the delightful feeling that I'm performing the superb landing. We taxi toward some tied-down planes, two of which are the Mustang and the Bearcat — lovingly restored, and perched like elegant antiques among the modern aircraft. Then, with Dave's coaching, I take off, correcting some of the mistakes I made leaving Danbury thirty minutes earlier. Once we're out of the Oxford pattern, Dave says, "Find Danbury." I blithely turn toward Bridgeport, realize my error after checking the heading indicator and compass, and set a new course for Danbury. Dave chuckles, and calls the Danbury tower for landing instructions; the controller's response is more crackling doubletalk to my ears.

On the final approach to Runway 26, over a congested area, Dave removes his hands from the controls and tells me to land the airplane. I tentatively apply landing flaps — an action that slows us down and adds lift — but I lose too much airspeed and flare out too soon. The stall buzzer sounds when we still have about twenty-five feet of air between us and the runway. "I'll take it," Dave says, and, smoothing out my blunders, he lands lightly and delicately once again. As we taxi to Bluebird, he tells me, "You did pretty good for a rusty pilot. There's just a lot of things you have to unlearn from the Piper Cubs and the Aeronca Champs. The Cessna's plenty different." He knows I'm hooked.

I ask him how long it will take before I can solo.

"If all goes well, you should solo after ten hours of dual instruction," he answers. "When do you want to have your next lesson?"

How about tomorrow, Saturday?

Dave says, "I think I'm all booked up for tomorrow, but call me in the morning. There's a lot of cancellation in this business."

Saturday, July 25, 1981
Danbury

THE weather is an exact duplicate of the previous day, as though no night had intervened. I have been thinking and dreaming flying for the past twenty hours or so, reliving every nuance of my sixty minutes in the Cessna 152. As soon as I finish breakfast, I call Bluebird. Sure enough, there is a cancellation, and I make an appointment for one o'clock.

At the airport, Dave informs me that we will be using another two-seat trainer, a blue-and-white Cessna 150 (N7682U), which is an older, less powerful version of the 152. It has a brand-new hundred-horsepower engine, however, which, Dave says, makes it almost as fast as the 152. Its speed doesn't really matter to me as long as it's an airplane. Dave watches me go through the pre-flight inspection, humming to himself and nodding approval of my diligence. Once we're belted into the cockpit, I decide to confess my feeling of obtuseness about radio communication. Why, I ask, am I so deaf to the radio talk, so unable to understand what the controllers are saying? Dave has obviously dealt with this problem before. "Look, first you got to realize that the people in the tower are there to help you, not to bug you," he says, as if explaining something to a child. "If you don't understand what they say, ask them to 'say again slower.' Don't be embarrassed. Also, listen carefully to the tower instructing others on that frequency, and you'll be amazed at the information you can pick up. If you know what to expect the tower to say, you can sort of understand ahead of time. When we call the ground control after we start up, they'll tell us the active runway, the wind direction and velocity, and the altimeter setting. If you expect that information, it won't sound so confusing. As for what you got to tell them, it's really simple: just tell them who you are, where you are, and what you want to do. Now try it for yourself."

I start the engine and maneuver the plane to the yellow holding line, at the edge of the nearest taxiway. I dial 121.60 on the radio — the ground-control frequency — and take the mike in hand, waiting for a clear opportunity to speak. The static and chatter stop for a moment, and I breathe deeply and say, "Danbury Ground, this is Cessna seven-six-eight-two-uniform holding at Bluebird Aviation. I want to proceed to the active runway." A withering reply comes back — a maelstrom of numbers and directions.

"Did you get it all?" Dave asks.

"A little," I answer. "I understood about using Runway Two-six and the altimeter setting, but I'm not sure about the wind stuff."

"Then call and ask again," Dave says. "And condense what you just said to 'Danbury Ground, Cessna seven-six-eight-two-uniform at Bluebird to active.' Keep it short and sweet. There are others waiting to talk, like on a party line."

I do as he says, and the patient ground controller gives me the same spiel at half speed. I comprehend everything. It works.

After the run-up at the end of Runway 26, I radio the tower controller on the proper frequency, 119.40, and advise him that Cessna 7682U is ready for takeoff. I am told — slowly — to wait for a Piper Cherokee to land and clear the runway. I forget to radio back the courtesy of confirmation — "Eight-two-uniform" — but Dave does this for me. When the Cherokee has landed and pulled off onto a taxiway, we shoot down the runway. There's that same exquisite thrill again, that extraordinary exhilaration. I want to yodel, or something. We leave the pattern and head for the practice area, where, at two thousand feet, Dave reacquaints me with the intricacies of slow flight and the reaction of the plane to varying degrees of flaps. At one point, Dave places an opaque plastic hood over my head, which allows me to see just the instruments, and tells me to hold the heading 320. Staring intently at the heading indicator, I manage to hold that course, more or less. "Now shut your eyes and hold that heading," he commands. It's impossible. At last, he says, "OK, now open your eyes and look where you are." The airplane is all over the sky — nose down, left wing dipping, forty degrees off course. Dave says, "You see, it can't be done. Blind men can't fly. Remember that."

We turn back toward the airport. Over Lake Candlewood, I call the tower for landing instructions. The tower advises me to enter the pattern for a landing on Runway 26 via the right base leg — something I've never done before. I am flustered, forget again to confirm, and enter the pattern at twelve hundred feet of altitude instead of the regulation fifteen hundred. But because I am so low and have a good glide angle I make a smooth approach and landing, with no flaps needed. Dave is pleased at my landing, but he criticizes me for coming in low and not using flaps. As for my failure to confirm the tower's instructions, he says, "Don't worry about that so much. Remember — first aviate, then navigate, then communicate." I have a heady sense of accomplishment in spite of my failings.

Back at the Bluebird office, three pilots are sitting around gabbing with Richard King. Pilots, like skiers and sailors, love to chat about their favorite occupation. Richard is talking about a former student of his who got exceptionally high marks on his private-pilot written test but didn't have a seat-of-the-pants feel for flying, which, Richard insists, is as important as knowing all the facts.

One of the other pilots comments, "Maybe that guy just has a photogenic memory." The others laugh before he can correct himself, but he takes it good-naturedly.

The conversation veers to the economics of running an instruction-and-charter service like Bluebird. When the Kings operated the Armonk Airport, they had six pilots working for them at one point, several of whom lived in the hangar and worked for free flight time, to improve their ratings. Some of them are well-paid airline captains today. Most of the Kings' Armonk income came from sightseeing rides — at two dollars and fifty cents a head — above the Westchester lakes and mansions. "On weekends, families would picnic at the airport and then they'd all go up for rides," Richard says. "No big deal then, everything was so cheap — a lot of inexpensive fun for a Sunday afternoon. Nowadays, with fuel so high, and with inflation and the state of the economy, it's all different. Charters can be terrible on the bottom line. The clients want the final cost, not the cost per hour, so if you run into bad weather or delays you make little or no profit. Right now, instruction and rentals are about eighty per cent of our income. But you have to enjoy what you're doing to be in this business. It certainly doesn't shower you with financial rewards. I always claim that you can make a small fortune if you start with a big fortune. Some charter operations and flight schools are being bought up by rich guys to dump money for a tax loss. I'll tell you, it's the best business in the world for dumping money — especially in the Northeast, with the weather we have."

This brings up the subject of hazardous flying in the Northeast. One of the visiting pilots says that was flying through a parachute-jumping area not far away when he was suddenly surrounded by dropping chutists. He landed at a nearby field and had to screech to a stop on the runway just as a grinning chutist plopped to a standup landing in front of his whirling propeller. Everyone tsks and shakes his head and is reminded of a similar stupidity. Finally, I must take my leave, first making an appointment for my third lesson.

Wednesday, July 29, 1981
Danbury

THE late morning is muggy and hot. Billowing clouds, looking suspiciously like thunderheads, are in the distant west, over New York State. Dave and I are above the Roxbury practice area once again, practicing slow flight, hundred-and-

eighty-degree turns, and landing-flap procedures, and I am doing well until the wind kicks up. There is practically no wind on the ground, but at three thousand feet the wind is unexpectedly strong, in irregular bursts. A storm front must be coming through. "Don't let that wind fly you," Dave warns, and he demonstrates how to turn into and out of the gusts.

On the way back to Danbury, at cruising speed, Dave orders me to close my eyes and put my head down while he performs crazy maneuvers — diving and climbing, turning abruptly this way and that. When he has finished with his fun, he says, "OK, open your eyes and find Danbury." I'm a little dizzy and disoriented but still sensible enough to recall that I was flying southwest before his shenanigans. I turn the Cessna until the heading indicator shows that I am flying southwest once again. But Danbury is nowhere to be seen. My intuition informs me that I am heading north, and when I check the magnetic compass my intuition is confirmed. I make the proper correction and spot Danbury. Dave is grinning. "Never trust an instructor when you're not looking," he says. "I changed the setting on the heading indicator to confuse you even more. Always double-check your course with the magnetic compass. Don't rely on just one instrument or sighting. Double-check everything. Imagine you see the word *assume* always spelled out on the windshield — a-s-s-u-m-e makes an ass out of you and me. Never assume."

I call the Danbury tower and receive clearance to land on Runway 26. This time, I understand almost all the instructions for entering the traffic pattern. However, there is another plane coming right at us, also entering the pattern. The controller didn't say anything about that. The basic rule of flying is still "See and avoid." Dave radios the tower and reports the other plane's position and asks to turn to avoid it. The controller diffidently grants the request. At last, we come in for a landing, which, mysteriously, is my best so far. It is so good, in fact, that Dave asks the tower for a touch-and-go and we take right off again. "I think you were just lucky," he says. We go around the pattern, and I land roughly, wandering off the center line, flaring out too soon, and stalling at about twenty feet. He is right. I was lucky. "Let's try it one more time," Dave says. We taxi back to the beginning of Runway 26 and, after tower clearance, I give it the gun. Halfway down the runway — at a speed of fifty knots, the wheels just off the ground — Dave pulls the throttle back to idle. "Your engine has failed," he tells me evenly. "Abort the takeoff." I am amazed at my coolness. I settle the plane onto the tarmac and keep it rolling straight until the speed slackens and I can safely brake it to a stop near the end of the runway. Dave is very playful today. "Nice," he says, and I am proud.

At the Bluebird office, Dave tutors me in a private ground-school session, in which we review procedures and regulations. I admit that I'm still having some trouble understanding the controllers on the radio. Dave suggests that I drop by the control tower one day to observe and listen to what goes on up there. "When you hear how others do it — and listen to their mistakes — it'll seem clearer," he says. "But don't put it off too long. The controllers are probably going out on strike soon."

Friday, July 31, 1981
Danbury

I TAKE Dave's suggestion and visit the control tower an hour before today's lesson. Despite the regimented confusion in that sunny, equipment-filled goldfish bowl atop a square concrete-and-steel stanchion at the northern intersection of the two runways, the welcome is friendly. Six of the fourteen controllers assigned to Danbury, including supervisors and trainees, are on duty when I arrive. A strike notice for August

3rd is posted on a bulletin board, but nobody mentions the strike or shows concern about it. The weather is clear and warm, and the Friday-afternoon traffic is heavy. A thin young man sorting out the air traffic speaks continually into his head-set microphone and shuffles plastic strips in a frame, each strip grease-penciled with an active aircraft's identification number. (Danbury does not have radar, so all air and ground traffic has to be controlled by sight and sound.) I soon realize that I am not the only one who is tongue-tied and obtuse on Frequency 119.40. One pilot flying through the control area within a five-mile radius of the airport has to be told several times about other traffic nearby. The phrase "Say again" is heard often enough to make me feel less idiotic. A trainee controller handling the ground frequency instructs a landing pilot to leave the runway on a particular taxiway, and the pilot leaves on the one directly opposite. The controllers take the pilot's mistakes in stride, with casual, gentle corrections — and vice versa, the pilots claim. These pressured technicians perform a tough job with spirit and efficiency. I understand them better now. They seem less godlike, more human.

When I meet Dave, he is in a surly mood. It turns out that a friend of his was badly hurt in a crash yesterday at Dutchess County Airport, near Poughkeepsie, when his engine quit as he was practicing an instrument approach. He barely missed some houses at the end of the runway. Dave's testy mood spills over onto me. It's hot, muggy, and buggy, and I am uneasy as we take off for some pattern work. On the third time around, we discover that the Cessna's radio receiver has stopped functioning. The tower can apparently hear us, but we can't hear it. "Well, that's the last straw," Dave mutters. He communicates our problem to the tower and asks for a green light, which is the visual equivalent of clearance to land — a system I recall from my old radioless Cub and Champ days. The tower understands our predicament. We spot a flashing green light beamed at us on the downwind leg and then a steady green on the final leg. I land with a small bump, and the radio receiver jumps to life, working perfectly. Dave groans, and says, "My idea of hell is to be flying somewhere surrounded by radios like this and they all quit, one by one." Since the radio can't be trusted, that's the end of today's flying.

In the Bluebird office, the talk is about faulty radios and the impending controllers' strike, set for Monday. The big question about the strike is whether the nonunion supervisors will continue to operate the Danbury tower or will be transferred to busier airports. Dave thinks that the Danbury tower will ultimately be closed down. "There are too many controllers here as it is," he says. "They may find out that they're not really needed, and be out of a job." My next lesson is scheduled for the following Friday, so I may not have to fret very much about controllers and towers and radios from now on.

Monday, August 3, 1981
Danbury

AT seven this morning, thirteen thousand members of the Professional Air Traffic Controllers Organization, or PATCO, go out on strike. I telephone Dave to ask him how things are at Danbury. "You'd never know there's a strike here," Dave says. "Three supervisors are keeping the tower open on a reduced basis, and maybe the others will return after Reagan's threat to fire them."

Friday, August 7, 1981
Danbury

I ARRIVE for my morning lesson and learn today from the talk around the Bluebird office that the Danbury tower was closed down the day before at 5:00 P.M. and is now "as quiet as a tomb." The decision was made by the Federal Aviation Administration, which transferred the three working supervisors to a higher-priority airport, in Bridgeport. Dave, who has been at a morning meeting of Danbury Municipal Airport operators, reports that there is a needless sense of panic among them. "It's silly," he says. "What did we do before there was a tower here? We flew just like it tells you in the book: airplanes should land and take off into the wind, only one airplane should be on a runway at a time, you should report your position, and you should obey all the rules. If everyone cooperates, we'll survive just fine." By general agreement, each pilot is broadcasting "in the blind" over the tower frequency of 119.40, informing anybody who's listening ("Danbury traffic") of his identification number, his position, and his intention. This expedient measure has been working fairly well so far, most pilots being doubly courteous and patient with their fellows. Of course, as in any case of spontaneous anarchy, the good behave better and the bad worse. A few hot-shots are taking advantage of the sudden lack of supervision, like children when the teacher suddenly leaves the classroom. Richard tells me that just after the tower closed down yesterday some hot-shot took off in his powerful plane, climbing almost straight up, "so you could read the numbers on top of his wings from the ground," and booming out of the pattern toward his destination without warning a soul. "He's a clear hazard," Richard says. "An accident waiting to happen. They come out of the woodwork at a time like this."

A brisk wind is blowing from the north, so we liberated fliers are using Runway 35, just in front of Bluebird. It is a difficult runway to land on, I have heard by way of airport scuttlebutt, because one's approach must be made between two wooded hills and over a pond, and these tend to generate odd wind currents and downdrafts. (Every airport seems to have its difficult runway, creating its own if-you-can-land-on-that-you-can-land-anywhere legend.) Perhaps because of my edginess about the absent controllers and the forthcoming landing on Runway 35, my flight begins badly, embarrassingly. During the run-up, while testing the magnetos, I flick the ignition switch too far to the left, to the "off" setting. *Bang!* A cannon-blast backfire. Dave and I both jump in our seats, our safety belts notwithstanding. Dave shakes his head. "Don't let it get you." he says, "I did it one day when I wasn't thinking. I thought I was shot. Worse was the shame. Just do it this once and never again."

Broadcasting in the blind to "Danbury traffic" is spooky. Some pilots are still calling the silent Danbury tower, and they have to be informed by whoever is listening that the tower is closed. When all appears clear, I radio, "Danbury traffic, Cessna seven-six-eight-two-uniform departing three-five." The ensuing hour of takeoffs and landings around the pattern is marked by one depressing error after another: shaky ascents, shakier descents, forgotten procedures, jerky maneuvers, sloppy control. When the hour is blessedly over, I ask Dave, "Where did I go wrong?" He responds with a long critique of my lingering old habits, my lack of concentration, my sudden nervousness, my run-up blunder. "But don't worry," he says. "It will come to you. This often happens to students after about five hours of instruction. There's just too much to think about, and so they forget everything. It's a question of getting the right feel of it once and for all."

I'm beginning to wonder if I ever will — if I'm too old to learn new tricks.

Sunday, August 9, 1981
Danbury

IT's an iffy day for flying, with a morning fog slowly diffusing into a dense summer haze. Dave sniffs the moist air and proclaims that we can fly the pattern and "work on those landings of yours." That's all right with me; after Friday's debacle I need all the pattern practice I can get. In my waking and sleeping moments since Friday, I have been landing Cessna N7682U — sometimes flawlessly, sometimes disastrously — and I feel as if I have added at least a dozen hours to my flight time, imaginary though they are. Apparently, the phantom flying has paid off. My five takeoffs and landings this morning, on Runway 26, are generally clean and smooth, with only a few flagrant errors. "You're doing real good," Dave says after my second landing.

"It feels good," I tell him. "The airplane seems like a part of me." I hear myself calling the machine an "airplane," as professional pilots invariably do — not simply a "plane."

More fliers in the traffic pattern are taking advantage of the controllers' strike. One airplane flies catercornered from its downwind leg to its base leg in a heedless rush to land. Another comes straight in without entering the pattern at all. Even a hawk at fifteen hundred feet is taking advantage, circling in front of me tauntingly. "Another case of see and avoid," Dave says, and just when I'm about to avoid, the hawk soars off to my right. He adds, "They can do a lot of damage, those birds."

The better I fly, the pickier Dave becomes, insisting on fine-tuning my technique. At one point, he apologizes. I tell him that I don't mind — that I want him to be tough. And so he pulls two more tricks on me. During my third takeoff, when I've reached an altitude of a hundred feet he cuts the power and announces an engine failure and an aborted takeoff. I lower the nose and bring the airplane to a gentle landing on what's left to me of Runway 26. "Real nice," Dave says. "That was real nice." On the next takeoff, Dave unlatches the door to his right and says, "Your passenger door has come open. Fly your airplane and close the door without losing your passenger, yourself, and your airplane." I reach across his lap to slam the slightly ajar door shut. The Cessna banks sharply and then yaws to the right. I have inadvertently turned the wheel and depressed the right rudder pedal. "Fly your airplane," Dave commands, and, chastened, I correct.

At the end of this basically cheering hour, Dave conducts a ground-school session in the Bluebird office. There are several interruptions. A chunky man accompanied by a well-fed blonde enters and asks, with a heavy foreign accent, about helicopter flights over the area. Dave directs him to a nearby helicopter-charter service. "Must be a spy," Dave says after they depart.

A former Bluebird student drops by to say hello. "I see you still got old Cessna eight-two-uniform," he remarks, referring to what I've come to consider *my* airplane. "I spent a lot of hours in that thing."

Two free-lance flight instructors, friends of Dave's, come in to chat and tease Dave about his girlfriends, one of whom is of Italian descent. "Watch out, Dave," one instructor says. "I never knew an Italian girl that didn't want to get married."

A man who flies model airplanes for a hobby inquires about learning to fly the real thing. "I've got the itch and I have to scratch it," he says. Sounds familiar.

Finally, the interruptions cease, ground-school class is dismissed, and I make an appointment for early the following Wednesday morning.

Wednesday, August 12, 1981
Danbury

AT nine o'clock, a luminescent ground fog is just beginning to dissipate under a weak sun. There is no wind to speak of. When the sky above the airport is clear, Dave and I take off in the Cessna 150 for more pattern work, to see if my landings are as good as they were three days ago. Once airborne over Runway 26, we are both struck by the loveliness of the patches of ground fog clinging to the valleys and the ponds of Putnam County, to the west. "What do you say we leave the pattern and take a look at the fog lifting?" Dave asks. At fifteen hundred feet, I swing a forty-five-degree turn to the right and climb to twenty-five hundred. The terrain below is a slowly evolving Japanese painting, full of billowy swirls and delicate tracings. Dave and I appreciate the view in silence. At last, he says, "Beautiful. I never get tired of the beauty from up here. It's always changing, changing . . . OK, Burt, let's go back to Danbury and do some practicing."

For the rest of the hour, and six minutes over, my landings and takeoffs, with one exception, are good. As we taxi back to

Bluebird, Dave asks me whether I've made an appointment for the required pre-solo physical examination yet. That's a broad hint — I must be nearing the time for soloing. I am at once thrilled and slightly terrified.

IT is clear on the ground but hazy aloft this morning. The forecast calls for a front to move in with possible thunderstorms. The wind is capricious, and so the traffic pattern has been revised — informally, over the radio, by Dave. "When I changed it, you should've seen the traffic jam up there," he tells me. "But it had to be done. Too many students were landing downwind on Two-six. The wind was suddenly coming from the east, so I switched the active to Runway Eight.

Nobody was doing anything about it except me. That kind of thing is when I miss the controllers. If they don't come back soon, the FAA should sell advertising on the sides of the tower, or maybe make it into a motel."

I haven't realized how professional my radio technique has become until Dave compliments me during one of our pattern flights. "Hey, you're really getting cool on that thing," he says. My landings today are not so cool, however. The haze and the variable wind have given me a little anxiety attack. I'm "overcontrolling," as Dave puts it — abruptly and needlessly shoving the controls around. "Don't spoil a good thing," he keeps telling me. "Keep it smooth — smooth and coordinated. Relax. Have fun." The last time around, Dave encourages me to "get it all together and really grease it in." With intense concentration, I make an excellent approach, everything just right. "Splendid," Dave says. But then I botch the finale by flaring too high and banging the airplane onto the runway. The inherent drama of the grand climax of flight — the landing — is destroyed; it is as if Hamlet were to appear for his final scene dressed in a bathing suit, muttering one-liners in Hungarian. "Look, Burt, landing right is a very fine thing," Dave tells me. "You don't want to fly the airplane into the ground and you don't want to stall it too high." He holds his right thumb and forefinger a few inches apart. "Theoretically, that's where you want to stall the airplane — that high off the ground. Keep it flying as long as possible."

After the disappointing lesson, Dave and I go for coffee at Donut Time, across Route 7 from the airport, and at the counter he conducts an impromptu ground-school class in emergency procedures. He outlines what to do in case of engine failure, electrical malfunction, control-surface problems, carburetor icing, and fire. "The important thing with emergencies is don't blow them out of proportion," he says. "Ask yourself, 'Is my airplane flying?' Nine times out of ten, it is.

One guy I know was freaking out because his flaps didn't work. So what? You can land without flaps, the way you did with the Cubs and Champs. You'll walk away from it. If you can walk away from a landing, it's a good landing. Whatever troubles you encounter, chances are somebody else has gone through them and walked away. Airplanes are safer than cars. The most dangerous part of flying is the drive to the airport. You just hear more about airplane crashes, because they're still sensational news. Pilot error is the big thing to avoid. Aviation is changeable, and you always got to keep ahead of yourself and everybody else."

Wednesday, August 19, 1981
Danbury

FLYING today is strange for two reasons: it is an ordinary midweek morning, but the Danbury traffic pattern is full of aircraft; and, while there isn't a breath of wind at ground level, at fifteen hundred feet tricky gusts from the north jiggle the Cessna around as if it were a balsa-wood toy. Both circumstances make me more edgy than usual, but, with Dave's comforting advice, I manage an hour's worth of fairly decent takeoffs and landings. Indeed, I am doing a lot better this morning than some other fledglings — especially a helicopter student who is trying to hover over a grassy practice area near the deserted tower and dips and slides alarmingly. I even muddle through another one of Dave's tricks. During a final approach, he pulls back the throttle to idle and announces, "You just lost your engine. Now put us on the runway." I set the airplane down gently with plenty of room to spare. Not bad, I think. "Not bad," Dave says.

Later, we see a tiny, sparkling Pitts Special S-1S — an aerobatic one-seater — rise crazily into the air after an abbreviated takeoff run. We are both agog with admiration and envy. Dave clucks, and says, "Man, that's flyin'! Every pilot should have one of those to unwind with after a tough day." Inspired, I guess, by the Pitts Special's performance, I proceed to make the best landing of my erratic career. "Get your medical," Dave says curtly.

As soon as I arrive home, I make an appointment for Friday with a local doctor qualified to give flight physicals.

Friday, August 21, 1981
Danbury

TODAY is a superb day for flying — a soft northwesterly breeze, a sky so clear that, as some pilots like to say, "you can see for five hundred miles." But my aviatic concern today is in the Danbury Hospital Emergency Department, where I fill out a long FAA application form and am examined by Dr. George Terranova for my third-class medical certificate. The application is detailed in the extreme, requiring particulars on flight time, old ailments, current ailments, physical and moral deficiencies such as drug addiction, alcoholism, arrests, and accidents, and even one's military dog tag number. The examination is equally thorough, with the usual corporeal explorations and heavy emphasis on vision and hearing acuity. I pass, to my immense relief.

Dr. Terranova is the head of the Emergency Department, and he uses his office there to conduct FAA flight physicals. During the Vietnam War, he was a flight surgeon in the Air Force, and he spent about nineteen hours a month in military aircraft. He gave up flying when he realized that he wouldn't have the spare time in civilian life to practice his aviating skills. He tells me, "Not flying regularly is like being away on vacation for a week and not driving your car. When you get behind the wheel again, the car seems strange to you. In a plane, that could be bad." He asks me how things are going at the Danbury Airport since the controllers' strike. I answer that things are fairly normal except for a few crazies. "Some people do go a little crazy when they're flying a plane — even some doctors I know," he says. "Once, I flew to Nantucket in a light plane piloted by a neighbor of mine, an airline captain. He told me he prefers to fly his plane in bad weather, because most of the nuts stay on the ground then. Anyway, good luck with your flying." He signs my medical certificate — a yellow card — and hands it to me. There is space on the back of the card for endorsements by my instructor that I am qualified to solo in particular makes and models of aircraft. When I solo and Dave makes the proper endorsement, the yellow card will become a student-pilot certificate as well.

Wednesday, August 26, 1981
Danbury

HEARTENED by my medical certificate and a swelling sense of confidence, I am ready to solo, if so bidden. I set out for my nine-o'clock appointment at the airport with a song on my lips and a veritable aria in my heart. When I arrive at Bluebird, I see a beaming, stocky young man parking Cessna N7682U. I learn that his name is Joe Ursone, that he is seventeen, and that he has just soloed for the first time. Dave and the others are congratulating him with pats on the back and high praise. "Joe really greased it right in," Dave says, with the pride of the trusting, vindicated master. "Three beautiful landings." I feel both happy for Joe and jealous of him. When Dave tells me later that "kids pick up flying real quick," I feel almost insulted. I want to ask, "How about *former* kids?" But I don't. Also, I don't mention the possibility of soloing today myself. Dave says that we'll do some power-off and power-on stalls if the ceiling is high enough under the thickening clouds. This brightens me a bit: stalls are the only maneuvers I haven't practiced for my soloing requirements.

While I am pre-flighting the Cessna 150, Dave describes an

accident at the airport over the weekend. "A guy landed with his feet down but his wheels up," he says. The pilot was unhurt, and his airplane was only slightly damaged, but when the crash trucks were at the scene on the runway another airplane landed and had to swerve onto the grass to miss the trucks and the crippled airplane. "The press is making a big deal out of it," Dave adds. "They're claiming it wouldn't have happened if controllers had been in the tower. Maybe yes, maybe no. Controllers are supposed to look out for such things as wheels-up landings, and warn other airplanes off after a crash, but who knows if they could have prevented that mess?"

As it turns out, the ceiling is too low to practice stalls, and that means I won't solo after all. There's barely enough usable altitude to perform takeoffs and landings in the pattern. My landings this morning are tentative and mercurial. "Why did you blow that one?" Dave shouts. "You were doing great until the very end!" A student pilot in another Cessna 150 bounces around on a landing, and I'm comforted once again to see that I'm not the only bumbling student around — young Joe Ursone notwithstanding. This knowledge moves me to finish off the lesson with two nice landings. "Good," Dave says at the end of the session. "Your last two landings were good and safe, but you still need more finesse, more fine-tuning."

OK, but when am I going to solo? Well, perhaps this very afternoon. In the Bluebird office, a student phones to cancel a three-o'clock appointment, which I snatch up. "If the ceiling lifts, maybe we can get some stalls in," Dave says tantalizingly.

By three o'clock, the sky has changed to bright blue with high, puffy clouds — good for stall practice. Before Dave and I go up in the Cessna 150, he invites me for a Coke at a roadside stand near the fairgrounds and proceeds to tell me the story of his life. Our roles are instantly reversed: I take my

logical place as the sage older man, and he becomes the confused youth. He tells me how he was infatuated with airplanes
at the age of thirteen, when his family moved to Ridgefield,
Connecticut, from New Jersey. His father took him to Bluebird Aviation for sightseeing rides and later for instruction.
On his sixteenth birthday, he started working at Bluebird as a
line boy, washing and gassing aircraft in exchange for cut-rate
lessons. His first instructor was James King, Richard's father,
and his second was Richard himself. Dave's interest in flying
waned during an unhappy stint at New England College, in
Henniker, New Hampshire, but after he graduated he went
back to aviation with a vengeance, finally winning his commercial and flight-instructor ratings at the Embry-Riddle
Aeronautical University, in Daytona Beach, Florida. After
working as a busboy and a car salesman ("I was the best damn
car salesman you ever saw"), he came back to Connecticut in
1979 and was hired by Richard as a flight instructor — a position that helps him gain flying time, experience, and advanced
ratings toward his goal of someday becoming an airline jet
pilot. But that dream seems to be evaporating. "The airlines
are laying off more pilots than they're hiring," Dave tells me
gloomily. "It's not like it used to be, when they'd take a
chance on a young pilot and pay for his jet training. Even
getting a job with the little commuter airlines is hard. It looks
dismal everywhere. People my age are getting awful fed up.
In three years, I'll be thirty, and then it will probably be too
late for a good career. I may have to go to Australia for a decent
airline job." Meanwhile, at Bluebird he is overworked in the
summer and underworked in the winter, and there are always
money problems. "This instructor business is rough," he con-
cludes, thoroughly depressed by his outpouring. I find that in
my new role as counsellor I can offer no substantial advice —
just useless sympathy.

Later, while we are belting ourselves into the Cessna 150,

Dave, still dispirited, points to the instrument panel and says, "What I should do is put a little rack with my toothbrush and shaving stuff here and never leave. That's how much time I spend in this thing during the summer." The cockpit looks like home to me, too; I've been in here a lot today. It's muggy hot, and we open the vents and the windows while taxiing to take off. Once aloft, however — and climbing to three thousand feet over the Housatonic River — both of us are refreshed and stimulated by the cool air and the startling views. Dave's mood has changed. "Well, sometimes the tension and work get to me," he says. "But it's always a new challenge up here. You leave your troubles on the ground." That's a hoary sentiment but nonetheless true. It's wonderful just to fly.

I recover ably enough from the stomach-lurching power-on and power-off stalls over the Roxbury practice area. The recovery procedures are the same as in the Cub and the Champ, so the technique comes to me easily. On our way back to Danbury, we fly directly over my house. With the strong sun illuminating my property, I am astonished at how clearly every familiar detail stands out. There are my son and my dog in the back yard, looking skyward. I rock my wings in salute, and my son waves. I spot a neighbor lounging in the buff beside his swimming pool, and there's another friend mowing his lawn on a tractor. Is that my favorite tennis partner on the town courts? My God, this is fun! It's a fantasy of a celestial view of the world come true. I've almost forgotten about soloing. What the hell. I'll do it some other sunny, bright day.

Friday, September 4, 1981
Danbury

SEVERAL less than sunny, bright days have kept me from my compulsive pursuit until this Friday afternoon of the Labor

Day weekend. Even today, the weather is rather uncooperative: a low mist slowly lifting, the ceiling just high enough for pattern work — not good conditions for a student pilot to go up alone. Another setback: the Cessna 150 is sidelined because of a broken carburetor linkage. Dave says we'll use the brown-and-white Cessna 152 — the first Bluebird airplane I flew, on July 24th. The 152 seems both familiar and strange to me. I have an uneasy feeling about this day.

After more than a week of being earthbound, I'm a little rusty, so perhaps it's just as well I don't solo. I recall what Dr. Terranova told me about the necessity of regular practice to be a skillful pilot. My worst error on our first time around the pattern is a final approach that's too fast. "You let your airspeed get away from you," Dave says after we land. "Trade some altitude for airspeed and use more flaps."

During the second landing, I do as he instructs, depressing

the flap lever to twenty degrees as soon as I'm lined up with the runway. I'm concentrating for all I'm worth when suddenly I hear a dull but loud "WHUMP!" coming vaguely from my left. My first thought is that I've hit a bird — a large bird. "What was *that?*" I ask as the Cessna yaws sharply to the left.

"I got the airplane," Dave says brusquely, and I take my hands and feet off the controls. We're still yawing left, veering toward the deserted control tower. Dave is intensely looking everywhere at once. With a gentle, delicate touch, he coaxes the airplane back over the runway. His concentration is awesome. I tighten my safety belt and harness, reasoning that if we have a rough landing at least my head won't smash into the instrument panel. Also, I shut up and keep out of Dave's way. Our letdown onto the runway seems to take forever, but Dave isn't rushing it. He is talking to the injured machine through his hands and feet, persuading it to respond rationally. We're coming in fast, a bit crookedly. Just before we touch down, Dave asks, "Your seat belt tight?"

"Yes," I answer, double-checking.

The stall buzzer buzzes, the tires squeal, and Dave says, "We're down."

I exhale loudly and whisper, "Beautiful."

He brakes and turns off onto the nearest taxiway. "Look at your left flap," he tells me.

I look, and see that it is still in the up position, while the right one is down. So that's why we yawed to the left. "Did it stick, or what?" I ask.

"I think it just broke," he answers. "That's what that sound was. The metal control arm must've snapped." He moves the flap lever to the "up" setting, and the right flap moves and freezes in place. "Yeah," Dave says.

"I checked the flaps in pre-flight."

"Well, those things happen," he says. "Remember what I once told you about aviation being changeable?"

I ask him if this has ever happened to him before.

"I've had both flaps stick down on me," he answers. "But that's not as bad as this. With one flap up and other down, we could've gone into a spin, and we didn't have much altitude to recover from a spin — which is why I took over from you."

"You were terrific," I tell him. "I thought we hit a bird. What if I was flying solo? Could I have brought it in to a decent landing?"

Dave smiles, and says, "I'm sure you could have, but it wouldn't have been one of your better landings. In something like this, the first thing you want to do is fly your airplane. Then it's a matter of bringing the airplane down in one piece. In a way, it's good when something like this happens once in a while — and you can walk away from it — because it makes you more careful about your flying habits and better prepared for the unexpected. A lot of your reaction is instinct, which is an amazing thing. You do what you feel is right. Of course, we had plenty of runway to land on and no crosswind, which was lucky."

I congratulate him on a brilliant performance, and he shyly looks away. For all my apparent composure, I am a little shaken once I set foot on the ground. Things slip inexplicably from my fingers. I keep thinking, What if I had soloed today?

Dave writes in my logbook, "Flap malfunction on landing. Burt remains 'cool.'" As he hands me my logbook with that ringing notation, he apologizes for the aborted lesson. "Gee, I was just about ready to hop out," he says — meaning that I would have likely soloed today after all. Now, with both Cessna trainers disabled ("It looks like the Libyan Air Force around here," Dave says) and the weather worsening, I'll have to wait a while longer.

Wednesday, September 9, 1981
Danbury

THE morning sky is the very definition of cerulean — autumnally impeccable. The murky, wet weather of the Labor Day weekend was blown to sea last night by a front moving down from Canada, but with the front have come strong, variable winds — perhaps too strong and variable for soloing. However, while I'm driving to the airport I hear on the car radio that this is the last "square-root day" of the twentieth century, being 9/9/81. Maybe a good omen.

At Bluebird, Richard tells me that the Cessna 152 turned out to have a broken cable leading to its left flap. "I never saw that before, even with much older airplanes," he says. "The hardest thing will be getting the replacement part, not fixing it." The Cessna 150, my old friend N7682U, is in good shape, the carburetor linkage having been repaired. It's nice to be back in the 150's cockpit, as familiar to me as my own living room. I trust this airplane more than the 152 — with good reason, I guess. With extra care, I pre-flight while Dave sniffs the wind and frowns. We start out on Runway 26, the wind seemingly favoring that strip more than the northerly, and infamous, Runway 35. In mid-pattern, the wind abruptly changes direction, blowing from due north in unsettling gusts. Under Dave's tutoring, I handle this situation by crabbing into the wind. "Nice, real nice, Burt," Dave says as we land crosswind, scattering some seagulls that have nonchalantly alighted on the runway.

The pilot of a Piper Cherokee radios that the wind is now favoring Runway 35 and that he is taking it on himself to change the traffic pattern. "He's right," Dave says, and we taxi to the beginning of Runway 35 for a takeoff. The letdown approach to Runway 35 is the one between two wooded hills and a pond; a pilot must stay high over the hills to avoid tricky downdrafts, and then descend steeply with full flaps onto the runway. Everything is going fine as we touch down until a green-and-yellow Bellanca, on a taxiway to our left, suddenly begins to cross the runway on a sure right-angle collision course with us. Dave takes the controls and swerves to the right, neatly averting the collision. It is the second near-accident in two flying days, but I feel more anger than fear. I spot the culprit's identification number and report it to Dave while he brakes the Cessna.

Dave grabs the microphone and radios, "Hey, Buster, you ought to really watch it there!" No response from the Bellanca, which proceeds to the end of Runway 35 for takeoff.

An anonymous voice on the radio says, "Are they keeping you on your toes today, Dave?"

"Did you see that one?" Dave replies into the mike.

"Yeah, crazy," the voice says.

"That guy in the Bellanca doesn't have his damn radio on," Dave tells me. "He never saw us. No reflexive braking, no beacon light, no nothing. If you follow him wherever he's going, you'll see he'll screw everything up." Dave is angrier than I am, and just as disconcerted. "Let's call it a day," he says as we taxi. "The wind is too tricky anyhow. Next time, we'll fly very early in the morning, before the wind kicks up. We'll be out here by ourselves, and we won't get run over. That incident was a little bit closer than I like." Same here.

Back in the Bluebird office, Dave holds forth on fliers like the one in the Bellanca. He says that that flier was not a serious pilot but, probably, a businessman with other things on his mind, like making his appointment in Syracuse or someplace. "That's the trouble with amateurs. All they're interested in is getting home or to their destination, not in flying properly. They make too many stupid mistakes. What we got to do in aviation is not just make the airplanes safer but improve the pilots." Somberly, we agree to meet at seven o'clock Saturday morning, weather permitting.

Saturday, September 12, 1981
Danbury

LAST night, after listening to the ten-o'clock weather forecast ("Coming up tomorrow, a hot, partly cloudy return to summer — a beach day"), I went directly to bed. I was sure, gut sure, that I would solo in the morning. Mentally practicing landings, I finally fell asleep at about ten-thirty.

I awake, brain crackling, at four o'clock, totally unable to close my eyes. The alarm goes off at five-thirty. First thing, I stare out the bedroom window. There is haze in the sky, a reddish sun trying to break through. "Red sky at morning, sailor" — and pilot? — "take warning." Everything is an omen lately. But there is almost no wind, and the haze will disappear once the sun gets higher. I eat a light breakfast, with two cups of coffee, and drive to the airport. It is only a quarter to seven when I arrive, so I have another cup of coffee and a sugared cruller at Donut Time.

Dave is waiting for me at the Bluebird flight line. Not another soul or machine is stirring. Dave is unusually formal and laconic. He informs me that the Cessna 150's tanks have

been topped off and that I should preflight the airplane scrupulously. In his usual manner, he sniffs the wind — or lack of
it — and tells me the runway we will be using: good old 26. I
sense that this is my day.

Everything must be perfect, I keep reminding myself. But
I am a little nervous. I have trouble attaching my harness
strap, which won't latch on to the safety belt. Dave hums
while I fiddle with the strap and prepare to start the engine.
Once it's started, I relax somewhat; the engine noise is comforting — a reassuring sound of tested technology. The radio
is quiet except for one other pilot, who is announcing to the
world at large that he will be flying into the Danbury traffic
pattern. While we hold before taking off, he touches down —
a clean, feather-light landing. The sun comes out strong, and
the haze immediately disintegrates. In fact, there is a harsh
glare, and, searching unsuccessfully in my shirt pockets for
my sunglasses, I realize that I have left them in the car. Damn.
Stupid. Everything must be perfect.

When the other active airplane has cleared the runway, I
radio my intentions and take off. On the downwind leg, I
unaccountably lose three hundred feet of altitude, but I correct and make a tight landing on the first third of the runway.
"Let's go," Dave commands, and we take right off again — a
touch-and-go. "Did you have your Wheaties today?" Dave
asks as we climb into the still air. "Your landing was fine, but
your approach was terrible. You were at twelve hundred on
your downwind leg. Now, make this one real good." With
heavy, sweaty intensity, I do just that — make a real good
landing. Dave compliments me and loosens up a bit, relating
the latest in airport gossip as we taxi back to the eastern end
of the runway. Like the most eager pupil in the class, I ask
him about iffy approaches. "If in doubt, don't," he replies. "I
always liked that expression: 'If in doubt, don't.'"

The third time around, Dave is still beside me in the cockpit. While I'm settling over the runway at two hundred feet, Dave orders, "Go around! There's nothing wrong with your approach. I just want you to go around." That's odd. Does this mean something significant? My ensuing pattern and landing are, as far as I can tell, unimpeachable. During the rollout, I think, My God, what does he want? I'm doing this as well as any student pilot. Silence while taxiing. Dave whistles, hums, whistles. As we pass the empty control tower, he says, "The tower people were over there yesterday, turning in their keys or something." More silence, more humming, more whistling. Then: "So what do you say, Burt? Do you want to take it around a couple of times?"

I can feel an enormous grin spreading over my face. "I'd be glad to," I answer.

"One rule of thumb: if you're in doubt about landing, go around again. But you should have no trouble." He points to a man fueling airplanes from a tank truck alongside the taxiway. "I'll hop out there," he says. "Make a full-stop landing and taxi back this way. If I signal you to go through the pattern again, just go. Enjoy it!" I stop near the tank truck, and Dave leaves the Cessna. We reach across his empty seat and shake hands.

"Thank you," I say.

"OK," he answers, and slams the door shut.

At last, I am alone, ready to first-solo for the third time in my life. I am sweating. I force myself to breathe deeply, to relax. I wiggle my toes. As I taxi away from Dave, I find that I am mumbling aloud. "OK, I'm going to solo," I say. "You've done it before. Nothing to worry about. Great weather. Just one other airplane in the pattern. I wish I had my sunglasses, that's all. But I'm going to enjoy it, as Dave said." While I hold at the end of Runway 26, I check all the instruments and make fine adjustments. Everything is all right. The other traffic has landed and pulled off the runway. The sky is clear of aircraft. The radio is broadcasting only muted static. "Danbury traffic, Cessna seven-six-eight-two-uniform departing two-six," I proclaim, pleased at the casual, if high-pitched, sound of my voice. I turn onto the runway, straddle the center line, and slowly push the throttle all the way in. The engine growls and then roars, and the Cessna rushes to a speed of fifty knots. Lighter by the weight of one man, it wants desperately to leave the ground, and I grant its wish by easing the yoke back. All by myself, I'm flying. It is, quite simply, the most exhilarating feeling I have ever known.

I hear myself talking: "Twelve hundred feet . . . cross-wind turn left to fifteen hundred . . . level off . . . cruising speed . . . downwind turn . . . Danbury traffic, eight-two-uniform downwind two-six . . . reduce speed . . . carburetor heat on . . . ten degrees flaps . . . seventy knots . . . turning base . . . turning final . . . more flaps . . . power off . . . line up on runway . . . looking good . . . sixty knots . . . runway coming up . . . fifty knots . . . I'm in there . . . stall buzzer . . . flare . . . flare . . . flare . . . yoke back and . . . I'm down and rolling . . . *Yahoo!* I did it!"

I brake, turn off the runway, and taxi past some Canada geese, which stare at me with what I assume is admiration from fellow-fliers. Dave is standing beside the tank-truck man just ahead. He is smiling broadly, and he makes an "OK" sign with the thumb and fingers of his right hand. I hold one questioning finger up, and he nods several times. Then I repeat the first flight, feeling just as thrilled but more confident. As I come in for my second solo landing of the day, I see an airplane holding at the end of the runway — an addition to my audience. I try hard to perform as well as the first time, but there is a small bump when I touch down. Oh, well, I'm safely on the ground and taxiing back to Dave. The notion strikes me that flying is the ultimate ego trip — to know that you can cause an ungainly contraption to leave the planet and return again in one piece. It is an unalloyed personal triumph. That's what hooks you.

Dave gestures for me to return to Bluebird. He walks the hundred yards or so behind me. Richard is waiting as I park the Cessna and shut the engine down. He shakes my hand and says, "You're not supposed to let your instructor walk back all that way." Pilot humor.

Then Dave appears and shouts, "You really greased it right in, Burt. You did real nice." That was what he told young Joe Ursone after he had soloed.

My pleasure is instantly doubled. I natter on about how good it felt. The others are indulgent. With some ceremony,

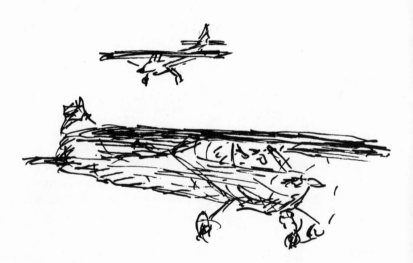

Dave endorses my medical certificate — now my pilot's license — and signs my logbook, adding the notation "Supervised solo — nice job!" The morning is warm and sunny. Life is beautiful. I am in rapture, for I am a pilot again, a kid again.

WELL, what now?

I have first-soloed for the third time in my life; I possess a student-pilot license, again for the third time; I have surmounted what looked at times insurmountable. I am a pilot again, all right, and maybe I feel like a kid again, but I am no kid in point of fact. Should I do what too many others have done after the first solo: pack away the logbook in the old memory chest and thenceforth fly only in jet airliners? Or should I hang in and try for a private pilot's ticket — a quantum leap beyond the first solo? Being a licensed private pilot means all kinds of new aviatorial freedoms and pleasures, like taking passengers along on cross-country trips. It also means dogged practice, study, and passing the written examination and the fearsome flight test given by a federal examiner.

A few days after that splendid September Saturday in 1981, when the headiness of my stellar accomplishment had worn off somewhat, I asked myself some hard questions, and I responded, with incautious middle-aged determination, that I would press on and earn my private license.

The watershed decision having been made, I phoned Dave Smith and informed him that I wanted to start all over again, as it were. From September 20th on, we embarked on a stern regimen of practice and study in the increasingly familiar airplane called N7682U, when the weather permitted. On local hops and cross-country flights, Dave put me through the rigors of navigational techniques — dead reckoning, pilotage, and the miraculous avionic methods; through the intricacies of flight planning; through the horrors of right and left crosswind takeoffs and landings; through the confusions of pilot-tower radio procedures; through the tricks of simulated short- and soft-field takeoffs and landings; through the chilling perversities of cold-weather flying; through lurching stalls of all durations and configurations; and through some sweaty voyages, at the end of which I was astonished to find that I had actually arrived at my appointed destination. Occasionally, when the air was calm and the sky was bright, I would solo the Cessna 150, practicing what Dave had preached. Those hours alone in the little airplane were heavenly rewards.

On one of our cross-country journeys, early in the new year of 1982, we blundered into a small emergency. It was a seemingly harmless flight from Danbury north to the airport at Great Barrington, Massachusetts, under a broken five-thousand-foot cloud layer. But no sooner had we touched down at Great Barrington than the cloud layer deteriorated into freezing rain.

"Let's get out of here," Dave said, and we took right off. At three thousand feet — heading south, Dave a watchful coach over my flying — we encountered a local snow squall. Its effect on me was traumatic. The kaleidoscopic flakes cut the visibility to nothing. Not even the wing tips could be seen in the blinding swirl. Ice was on the struts, and probably on the control surfaces. The RPM dropped until the carburetor heat was placed in the full-on position. I was downright scared. Dave was phlegmatic.

"Here's a good chance for some instrument work, Burt," he said, "and without a hood. Look at your instruments, not out the windows. Trust those dials, not your senses. If you rely on your senses, we'll be in a spin before you know it. It's hard not to react to your senses, but you got to force yourself. We should be out of the snow in a minute or so. It's just a little squall."

With my eyes fixed on the instruments, I managed to hold the airplane on course and keep the wings fairly level. From time to time, Dave would nudge the yoke, correcting one of my intrusive sensory errors. Onward we plowed through the snow toward, I hoped, Danbury. The little squall was getting bigger, if anything.

Dave studied the situation and said, "Let's call Poughkeepsie and get a DF steer, so we can find out exactly where we are and the shortest way out of this stuff." I knew that a DF steer (DF standing for "Direction Finder") is a radio procedure in which an appropriately equipped Flight Service Station can track a lost airplane on an electronic screen by receiving its radio signal. The Poughkeepsie FSS, at Dutchess County Airport, was right on the ball. By tracking designated clicks of our microphone button and voice transmissions, the specialists there plotted our position. They gave us a new heading, out of the snow squall and straight to Danbury. I was pleased to note that we weren't terribly far off course.

After we landed and shut down the airplane at Danbury — the weather the same as when we took off (O fickle New England!) — we heard a loud dripping sound from the engine cowling. Its source was a large chunk of ice, melting from the engine heat and the above-freezing temperature at land level.

"Gee," Dave said, fingering the water, "it was worse than I thought. Good thing the carburetor heat was working. Well, at least you know what to do if you fly into a snow squall again." I told him I wasn't planning to fly into a snow squall again — but then, you never know.

BEFORE long, it was time for my first solo cross-country flight, an extended hop of sixty-three nautical miles from Danbury to the Windham, Connecticut, airport and back again to Danbury — a round trip of about two hours. Done and done. But before I could execute my second solo cross-country flight, I had to sit out some filthy winter weather. My missions were scrubbed with frustrating frequency, and I was getting rather edgy — to say nothing of rusty — as the sleety, snowy weeks slipped by. A couple of breaks in the storm clouds allowed me to practice locally, solo and dual, thus preventing my rustiness from becoming total corrosion. Finally, in late April, I successfully flew solo, round trip, between Danbury and Columbia County Airport, in upstate New York. Two solo cross-country flights down, one super solo cross-country — with three legs, including a two-hour stint — to go.

Then, in early May, Dave Smith suddenly quit his job as an instructor with the Bluebird Aviation Corporation, having won a position as co-pilot for a small commuter airline. He had taken the first step toward his restless dream of being a jet airline pilot. (Not long thereafter, he would be hired by American Express as a corporate jet pilot.) I, of course, was happy for Dave, but his abrupt departure from Bluebird was something of a setback for me in my own little restless dream of becoming a private pilot. It meant starting over again with a new instructor — one, perhaps, who wouldn't understand my peculiar failings as Dave had, or one, perhaps, who taught by another technique.

As good luck would have it, Richard King, the owner of Bluebird, took over my tutelage. Rich had once instructed Dave, so the changeover was untroubled. Indeed, Rich's maturity and professionalism raised anew my spirits and dedication. In our first dual session, when we reviewed the entire curriculum of flying a light airplane, Rich's criticism was terse and direct. Later, on the ground, he outlined precisely what I had to master in order to earn my private ticket, and together we planned a course of action: the big solo cross-country, night flights, stalls, 720-degree steep turns, slow minimum-control flying, instrument work under the dreaded hood, navigational and emergency procedures, aeronautical knowledge for the written test, flight-proficiency practice and more practice. We flew the Cessna 150 long and hard together, and then Rich would hand over the airplane to me, saying, "OK, instead of me yelling at you, go up and do what we just did all by yourself." I could honestly feel that I was getting better all the time.

Throughout the long, hot New England summer of 1982, I practically lived in N7682U, discovering that summer haze could be as disconcerting as winter snow. On one murky solo jaunt in June, warming up for my long cross-country, I became disoriented somewhere over northern Westchester County, but I found my way back to the Danbury Airport by happening upon Interstate 684 and following the dim automotive traffic north. I was one happy student pilot when my landing gear touched down on the Danbury asphalt.

That summer of my discontent was crowned by the big solo cross-country flight — from Danbury to Glens Falls, New York, to Pawtucket, Rhode Island, and back to Danbury. Everything was going fine until, on the long second leg over southern Vermont, the sea-borne haze thickened to pea soup and my single electronic navigation aid (a VOR, or Very High Frequency Omnidirectional Range, receiver) went on the blink. My next destination — North Central State Airport, near Pawtucket — was nowhere to be seen. Running low on fuel, I nervously skirted the busy Providence terminal area and headed for what I knew was Long Island Sound and the less hectic Groton–New London Airport. After I landed at Groton, I had the airplane refueled and asked a man on the airport staff to sign my logbook. He perused me, my eyes probably as hazy as the atmosphere, and wrote "Arrived alive" next to his name. I flew the third leg back to Danbury by following the northern shoreline of the Sound and hooking a right turn west of Bridgeport. Rich was comforting; he told me that I did the right thing by landing at Groton. One more giant hurdle cleared, sort of.

There followed some ground-school classes with Rich and others, and some sessions before a film-strip carrel that spewed out aeronautical information. The ground-school classes were helpful in illuminating some fuzzy areas, but the film-strip contraption was tedious, making me feel like a backward fifth-grader. I decided to plunge into a curriculum of individual study. I bought all the necessary books and manuals, sat down one night in front of the imposing pile, and started to read and underline. The trouble was, it had been about twenty-five years since I had intensively studied for an examination. I had forgotten how. Hundreds of tests of all kinds I had taken right up through graduate school, and now I had forgotten how to cram. There was no way out but to learn how all over again.

Meanwhile, some more changes occurred. N7682U disappeared from Bluebird's stable, its owner, who leased it to Bluebird, having decided to base it elsewhere. Rich checked me out in a venerable low-wing Beechcraft B-19 Sport, which was rather like switching from a Volkswagen Beetle to a 1970 Buick sedan. The Beechcraft Sport was certainly more substantial in turbulence and on crosswind landings, but lumbering and slow to the touch. "The sled," Rich called it. In the fall, Bluebird leased a Cessna 152 — N89044, by name — and I turned to it as to an old friend. N89044 would be my airplane from then on.

Another change. Rich sold Bluebird's name and equipment to the nearby Sadler Aero Center. The pressures of running a business seemed less preferable to him than free-lancing as a charter pilot, instructor, and FAA flight examiner. As he put it, "I'll be able to make up all that time I didn't spend with my wife and kids." For the last-phase cram course of instruction, he handed me over to Gene Robinson, who operated the Sadler Aero Center. "He's the best around," Rich said.

Again, Rich was right. Gene, an affable, gregarious man in his thirties, worked me hard (in his affable, gregarious manner) during that stretch drive to what I hoped would be the finish line. After each long lesson with Gene, when I left the 152's cockpit I was worse for wear but a measurably better pilot. He was particularly demanding about instrument proficiency, 720-degree steep turns, stalls, and emergency procedures. The optional night-flying privilege, requiring three hours of post-sunset flight with at least ten takeoffs and landings, was grueling, especially in the winter months: snow showers at night are positively hallucinogenic; the runway is never exactly where you think it is, landing lights or no; a full moon on a cloudless evening can be as blinding as the sun, and stars sometimes look like another airplane's strobe navigation lights. But night flying is also wondrous to behold, and I was glad that I had the valuable experience and aesthetic pleasure.

MY written test was scheduled for a Sunday morning late in January, at a certified examiner's house, in Ridgefield, Connecticut. For a week before the test, I drove friends and family alike half-mad with my compulsive cramming and my entreaties to them to quiz me on the massive technical data I was ingesting. They ended up memorizing almost as much as I had. On that forbidding, wintry Sunday morning, I was as tense as a college freshman taking his first midterm. Had I overstudied? Would I draw a big fat blank? Should I have quit grinding away the night before and gone to bed earlier? As it turned out, the heavy lucubration paid off; I finished the examination in less time than the allotted two hours and I was able to double-check my answers. Everything seemed to be one hundred per cent correct. A couple of weeks later, I received my grade from the FAA scorers in Oklahoma City: one hundred per cent. Not bad for a fifty-year-old born-again student.

I was riding high. The finish line was actually in sight. I ignored all other pursuits in order to fly as much as the weather would allow. Consumed by aviation, I relived and emended flying events in my sleep, at the dinner table, while shaving. Gene put me through an extended simulated FAA flight examination, covering everything he could imagine a real FAA flight examiner would ask for, and more. On March 14, 1983, he wrote in my logbook "Recommended for private pilot flt. test."

The time had arrived for the real FAA examiner to come forward, and he was none other than Richard King. On hearing this news, my first thought was, Is this good or bad for me? Certainly, Rich, as my former instructor, knew what kind of flier I was, knew my foibles and alleged skills, but would he take this knowledge into consideration during the test? Or would he be doubly demanding? I decided that Rich, true to his character, would be scrupulously dispassionate — and that was exactly what happened.

The flight examination was scheduled for March 19th, at nine in the morning, but a sinking ceiling scrubbed it. Since I showed up at the airport anyway, Rich took the opportunity to administer the oral part of the test. He loosed a barrage of no-nonsense questions at me. I answered and I passed. Two days later, there were possible icing conditions, and again the flight test was postponed. I was, by then, impossible to live with — jumpy, testy, unable to think about anything but the delayed appearance of the monster, the big exam.

My edginess wasn't improved any by a conversation with a friend and fellow-pilot, who told me that at his flight examination he traveled no farther than the end of the runway, never even getting into the air. He had been ordered to execute a short-field takeoff and had forgotten to apply ten degrees of flaps before he turned off the taxi strip. "That's it, let's go back to the tie-down area," the examiner had told him curtly. He had to wait a month for another try.

"With some examiners, only a perfect score is passing," my friend said. "Of course, when you finally pass muster, which I did on my second try, the first thing you think is, It's only right that it should be so difficult. The harder the better — especially for those who follow you."

On Wednesday, March 23rd, at nine in the morning, Rich and I went at it again. Earlier, I had telephoned the Poughkeepsie FSS for a weather briefing. The present conditions were a fifty-two-hundred-foot broken cloud cover, with visibility of twenty miles and a westerly surface wind of thirty-five-knot gusts. The forecast was for a lower ceiling, possible wind shear, and snow showers. To my astonishment, Rich said it was a "go." I was equally astonished at my calmness. I figured, What the hell, I'll give it my best shot.

With Rich scrutinizing my every movement, I plotted a cross-country flight to the Simsbury, Connecticut, airport, which Rich had chosen for the first stage of the test. I checked and rechecked everything, from Omnidirectional Range radials to Unicom frequencies. I preflighted N89044 as I never had before, the airplane and I both shivering in the bitterly cold wind. At last, Rich and I belted ourselves into our seats, and after I made sure that my passenger, so to speak, was properly harnessed and had securely closed his door, I started the engine. I cleared my voice several times before I dared radio the Danbury ground controller for instructions. We were assigned Runway 26, and Rich ordered a short-field takeoff. The cabin heater was beginning to thaw out my toes; the rest of my body was already bathed in perspiration, as if it were mid-July.

I performed a short-field takeoff, remembering to apply the ten degrees of flaps before turning onto the runway. Because of the ferocious headwind, it was a *very* short takeoff. I set a northeasterly course for Simsbury, fighting the westerly crosswind to maintain heading and altitude. Over Watertown, I announced my calculated ground speed of one hundred knots, whereupon Rich said quietly, "Forget Simsbury. Let's go to Bridgeport."

Bridgeport was directly to the south, barely visible on the horizon. I homed in on the Bridgeport VOR and struggled with the crosswind from my right, which did its best to shove the airplane to New Haven. I established a sharp crab and managed to keep the VOR needle centered. A few minutes of this and Rich said, "Forget Bridgeport. Give me a departure stall." I cleared the area with two ninety-degree turns and gave him a departure stall. Then, at his command, a full-flap landing stall. Then some maneuvering at minimum-controllable airspeed and some turns around a point, devilishly slippery in that wind. I had no idea of how I was doing, nor did Rich give me the slightest hint.

When I had completed my last turn around a point, Rich ordered a new course to the Pawling, New York, VOR. I obeyed, my head aswirl with changes of direction. Just north of Lake Candlewood, at an altitude of three thousand feet, he reached over and eased back the throttle to idle. "Emergency landing," he said. "You just lost your engine."

Now, I had gone through this training drill several times, and I knew that it was always different. One must immediately choose a likely field to set down upon, and then one must consider the best approach, always maintaining flying speed and taking into account the wind direction. Today, the wind was an enormous factor. I picked my field, a gently rolling sward beyond some power lines. I calculated that I could easily clear the power lines and slip in. But as I descended downwind to the field, I realized that I had too much altitude and I would probably overshoot, so I extended the final approach. The strong headwind helped. It would be a dicey landing but I would make it, in a pinch. At about five hundred feet, Rich pushed in the throttle to full and said, "Let's go back to Danbury."

Well, I thought, I guess I've flunked. To have come this far and failed! O cursed March day! Furious with myself, I was nevertheless determined to make the best landing of my career at Danbury. I called in to the Danbury tower for landing instructions and was informed that the active runway had been changed to 35, the north runway. The wind still seemed to be howling in from the west, but I didn't argue. Perhaps I should have argued. I soon discovered that it would be a severe, classic crosswind landing. Crabbing heavily to the west, buffeting in the gusts, attempting to line up with the center of the runway, I made my final approach between two wooded hills — notorious landmarks for Danbury pilots. Somehow, I held it all together to ground level and bounced on the airplane's left wheel, then straightened out for a long and bumpy roll. The sweat had trickled down my arms to my wrists, where it joined in startling confluence the sweat from my palms.

We taxied in silence. I didn't trust myself to say a word to Rich. At last, the silence was shattered. "You passed, as I knew you would," Rich said. "The emergency procedure was a little rough, but if you can handle an airplane in this wind, you deserve to pass." I shouted a self-congratulatory shout. I was in unadulterated ecstasy.

With my duly signed Temporary Airman Certificate (which gloriously read "Private Pilot/Airplane Single Engine Land") and with my brand-new logbook (which I had promised myself if I passed) and with a feeling of exhilaration unknown to mankind before or since (which bored to tears everyone I spoke to for days thereafter), I booked that dear, game airplane, N89044, for the following Sunday, when I would carry my first authentic passengers ever.

THROUGHOUT the remaining months of 1983, I took trusting family members and friends for dozens of rides. Their faith in my neophytic skills inspired me; one couple even offered their cherished five-year-old son as a guinea-pig passenger in the two-place Cessna 152. (Both parents and child did fine.) When I moved up to the four-place Cessna 172, it meant longer, faster, more comfortable trips for my passengers and myself. They enjoyed sharing my fun in flight; I enjoyed sharing theirs. Flying makes for mutually advantageous relationships.

I also flew more often with fellow-pilots, sometimes in their own airplanes. One colleague (if I may be so bold to use that term) was John Champlain, an American Airlines captain, who was a part-owner of a Bellanca Citabria aerobatic tandem two-seater. In the course of our casual hops to here and there, he introduced me to the thrills and wonders of aerobatics. High over the countryside we would loop and roll and spin, with John leading me through the intricate maneuvers until I almost believed that I was performing the stunts by myself. I became entranced with the perilous, rarefied world of aerobats, and I thought that an exceptional example of the odd breed might be somebody I'd like to write about. Jon Swan, a poet and friend who lives near Canaan, Connecticut, was suffering my wide-eyed tales of aerobatics one day when he suggested that I look up his neighbor Stanley J. Segalla, an exceptional aerobat if there ever was one. I did, and here is the result.

WHEN powered heavier-than-air flight began, in the first years of this century, the big trick was simply to remain airborne as long as possible. Of the four free flights that Orville and Wilbur Wright piloted on December 17, 1903, near Kitty Hawk, North Carolina — the first tentative excursions into the air by a man-carrying, engine-driven machine — the longest was an evanescent fifty-nine seconds. It wasn't until almost two years later, after a good deal of experimentation and tinkering, that the Wright brothers were able to keep their latest flying machine in the air for as long as thirty-eight consecutive minutes. During that remarkable flight, their airplane ascended and descended at the pilot's will, and, more important, it flew a circular course. It actually *turned*, and the second big trick had been performed.

Once the world realized that a flying machine could be directed — that it wasn't destined to go only in a straight line or to be shoved about by the wind's caprice — the possibilities seemed limitless. The "wondrous freak," as it was called, was suddenly more than just a dangerous hobby or an obsession; it had practical advantages, too. As aircraft controls and engines were improved — especially by the competitive European aviation pioneers — speed, distance, and carrying capacity increased. In 1909, Louis Blériot flew his skeletal monoplane across the English Channel from Calais to Dover in thirty-seven minutes, proving that airplanes could go from one point to another faster than, say, a ship. Another Frenchman, Henri Farman, flew his biplane on similar odysseys. The Farman biplane had a revolutionary innovation — primitive ailerons, or hinged sections of the wings, which enabled the pilot to bank and turn with comparative ease. Previously, airplanes could bank and keep their lateral balance aloft only by inefficient forced warping of the wings. The Farman system — a control stick for operating the elevator and the ailerons, and a foot bar for moving the rudder — became standardized, and it is basically the control system used in light aircraft today. The freedom that came with such control inspired the adventurers of early aviation to experiment with radical maneuvers; as a result, the art or sport or theatrics of aerobatics — aerial acrobatics — was born.

What these adventurers performed were called "stunts," and the "stunt fliers," with their attendant publicity, caught the public imagination and drew large crowds to their exhibitions. The stunt flier was aviation's equivalent of the daring young man on the flying trapeze, but his tricks were bigger and better. A disciple of the Wright brothers, Walter Brookins, helped found the Wright Exhibition Company, in 1910. Brookins thrilled audiences at fairgrounds with steep banks and spiral dives — commonplace maneuvers today, readily accomplished by every licensed private pilot, but considered then to be the acts of a madman. The Wrights' main American competitor, Glenn Curtiss, established a rival band of stunt fliers in Hammondsport, New York, his home town. The Curtiss Exhibition Company featured Lincoln Beachey, who was billed as the world's greatest aerial daredevil. Beachey was more showman than technician. His heart-stopping vertical plunges, from which he pulled out at the last possible second, and his airplane-vs.-automobile races against Barney Oldfield and Eddie Rickenbacker made him a rich man before he died, in 1915, when he ran out of airspace while attempting to recover from a dive over the Pan-Pacific Exposition grounds, in San Francisco. The public ate up such spectaculars, tragedy or no. Much of the draw was the distinct possibility that the frail aircraft and their harebrained pilots wouldn't make it down in one piece. The public was not often disappointed.

Meanwhile, the more serious, and less wealthy, aerobats were experimenting with equally perilous maneuvers, many of them unintentional. For instance, one day in 1911 a British pilot named Fred Raynham flew his Avro biplane through some British fog, became disoriented, and found himself in a dreaded spin. The spin — a stall that degenerates into an uncontrolled, whirling helix, with the airplane rolling, pitching, and yawing all at once — was the grand enigma of young aviation, a treacherous unknown that ended many a flying career. Raynham pulled out of the spin, but he didn't know how he had accomplished that feat. The answer came within a year, when another British pilot, Lieutenant Wilfred Parke, of the Royal Navy, managed to get his Avro biplane into similar straits. Parke's spin was to the left. With some remarkable instant experimentation, he applied rudder in the direction of the spin, which only tightened the helix. He then pressed the right rudder bar, and the airplane magically stopped spinning. Parke recovered control fifty feet above the ground, ultimately landing safely. He had solved the spin enigma for all time: use opposite rudder to the direction of the spin.

Pioneer aviators sometimes found themselves accidentally flying upside down, after wind gusts had flipped their flimsy craft over or they had misapplied the controls. Amazingly, the airplanes tended to right themselves from inverted flight. This anomaly led aerobatic pilots to consider attempting what seemed to be the impossible maneuver — the loop, in which the airplane sequentially passes through a climb, inverted flight, a dive, and a return to level flight. By 1913, looping had become the enigma to solve and an unofficial race was on to execute it successfully. The winner was an officer in the Imperial Russian Air Service, Lieutenant Peter Nikolaevich Nesterov. In August of 1913, he decided on his own to give the wild stunt a try. From an altitude of about eighteen hundred feet, he dived his seventy-horsepower Nieuport IV toward an aerodrome near Kiev, pulled back the control stick, felt the positive-gravity and centrifugal forces weigh down his body and draw the blood from his brain, hovered inverted, and recovered to level flight, thus describing a complete circle. He lived to tell the story — and to be reprimanded by the Czarist military for recklessness and endangering government property.

A Frenchman named Adolphe Pégoud was also flirting with the loop, in a fifty-horsepower Blériot. A month after Nesterov's unrewarded achievement, Pégoud performed exactly the same loop — in fact, several loops — before a horrified assembly at an aerodrome in Buc. He offered encores of a half-roll recovery, spirals, tail slides, an S dive, and, some claim, complete diving rolls. Like Nesterov, he lived to tell the story, but his reception on the ground was happier. He was an instant national hero, although the French military later banned "Pégoud-ing" after less talented imitators crashed. Both Pégoud and Nesterov were killed in aerial combat during the First World War. Pégoud, who was paid as much as nine thousand dollars a day for aerobatic displays, was an incorrigible hotspur right up to his death. He thought nothing of downing an entire roast chicken and a bottle of champagne before a performance, and he prepared for the stress of sustained inverted flight by having his Blériot mounted upside down on trestles and remaining strapped in the cockpit for long periods. He was one of the first French aces of the war, shooting down six enemy aircraft before he himself fell. Nesterov, equally impetuous, became an early battle casualty by deliberately ramming an Austrian airplane over Galicia.

Once word of Nesterov's and Pégoud's accomplishments had spread, "looping the loop" was all the rage. It was headline-making stuff for the showmen. To the public, the stunt was far more enthralling than new speed and distance records or new aircraft designs. At exhibitions throughout America, stunt fliers like Lincoln Beachey and Art ("The Boy Birdman of Ft. Wayne") Smith attempted consecutive loops, nigh-impossible outside loops (with the cockpit on the outside of the circle, rather than on the inside), nighttime loops with accompanying pyrotechnics, full rolls, spins, and skywriting. In Europe, there were the popular Ballet Aérien; the first aerobatic match for prize money; and special loop-the-loop exhibitions for potentates, the stunt fliers sometimes inviting comely chorus girls or celebrities like Winston Churchill along for the ride. The Europeans loved these flying circuses as much as the Americans did. Among the more dedicated spectators were the generals and armament-makers, who were about to go to war.

Suddenly, all the show-biz stunting paid off in ghastly practicality. The airplane proved itself to be a tool of war, first as a reconnaissance device and eventually as a fighter and bomber. Warplanes were designed, manufactured, and sent off to battle within the space of a few months; the Fokkers, Bristols, Spads, Handley Pages, Nieuports, Jennys, Sopwiths, Morane-Saulniers, the Avros quickly became legends as the machines and the men who flew them fell in frightening numbers. The stunt fliers of the prewar years were the instructors and aces in their nations' armies, and they lost no opportunity to invent new tricks: the Immelmann turn (an abrupt climbing turn); the English bunt (a half outside loop with a half-slow-roll recovery); the *vrille* (a quick spin to a new heading); the *virage* (a short inverted dive); and a variety of tighter, increasingly daring loops, rolls, spins, and inversions. After the war, the aces who made it home were the new heroes. All over the United States, Eddie Rickenbacker, Jimmy Doolittle, Carl Spaatz, and William Wellman, among others, were in demand at exhibitions to perform mock dogfights, formation aerobatics, and assorted stunts.

Aviation blossomed like ragweed in August. Engineers designed aircraft that were faster, bigger, and capable of flying longer distances than anyone had ever imagined possible, and pilots to test these airplanes became the new technician-aerobats. Still, the other side of aerobatics — stunt flying for thrills and profit — continued to titillate the public. With war-surplus Jennys available at bargain prices (more than ten thousand were produced during the war), any fledgling pilot could go into show business for himself, barnstorming at carnivals and selling short rides to the more intrepid rubes. Wing walking, rope-ladder pickups, ribbon cutting at ground level, wing-to-wing transfers, and even an aerial mock tennis game were the latest stunts — anything to shake loose good coin from the crowd. Just watching somebody loop the loop was no longer enough; flying-circus higglers promoted marathon looping. Up and up went the record for consecutive loops, until Charles (Speed) Holman topped it off with fourteen hundred and thirty-three in 1930. (It was said that eyelids tend to weaken after about a hundred loops, so some pilots would use adhesive tape to hold their lids up.) Madcap fliers were officially welcomed into the show-business fraternity as stuntmen for the movies. Dick Grace, a war pilot, literally broke his neck crashing crates into trees, rooftops, and other crates in the filming of William Wellman's *Wings*. Women, too, got into the act, demonstrating to adoring audiences the same derring-do as the men.

After Charles Lindbergh's solo flight from New York to Paris, in May of 1927, aviation took on a more sober demeanor. Government regulations, improved technology, and new job opportunities reformed a lot of stunt fliers into conscientious aerobatic aviators. The Germans were particularly keen on serious aerobatics, because the Versailles Treaty had restricted them to slow, basic aircraft; one way for the demilitarized Germans to keep up with advances in aerial tactics was to encourage their aerobats — among them Ernst Udet, a First World War ace and later a Luftwaffe general, and Rudolf Hess, whose ultimate stunt flight, to Scotland in 1941, astonished the world. Indeed, aerobats all over Europe were training for what was looming as the biggest international aerial competition of all. In America, Jimmy Doolittle was typical of the stunt flier turned aerobat. After earning a doctorate from the Massachusetts Institute of Technology, he involved himself in aeronautical research and testing, perfecting the difficult outside loop and helping to establish the fighter and the bomber as crucial instruments of warfare. When world war came again, the aerobats had refined their skill into a cruel art form.

Today, both military and civilian aerobatics must meet exacting standards. In international competitions, the complex Aresti aerocryptographics system delineates thousands of maneuver variations within defined airspace and assigns scoring points for each. With the continuing popularity of private flying (the high cost of aircraft and fuel notwithstanding), aerobatics has become a participant sport for many pilots. The barnstormers of today — working mainly in the West, where they put on impromptu shows in the desert — are viewed with a certain disdain by contemporary aerobats, who perform in severe competitions and at regulated air shows. Yet there's a bit of the show-biz spirit in even the most committed practitioners of the strange, perilous art — for instance, Stanley John Segalla, of Canaan, Connecticut.

STANLEY SEGALLA, who was fifty-nine years old when I met him in 1983, plies the trade of construction contractor, in partnership with his then twenty-four-year-old son, Billy. That's how they earn their money. But what both Stanley and Billy really like to do is fly small airplanes in fantastic configurations for fun at air shows, which have been on the upswing in recent years. They are two of the main attractions of Northeast Airshows, an aviation-packaging outfit — a sort of latter-day flying circus — that provides thrills for spectators at fairs and exhibitions from May through October. Stanley also does some free-lance flying, mainly at the Old Rhinebeck Aerodrome, in Rhinebeck, New York. For the past two decades, he has specialized in something called the Flying Farmer Act — an aerial vaudeville routine in which he plays the role of a hick dairy farmer who accidentally finds himself alone at the controls of a Piper Super Cub.

"The originator of the Flying Farmer Act is probably un-

known," Alan Loncto, the director and public-address narrator of Northeast Airshows, told me. "The routine has been
around for about fifty years. Everybody loves it — especially
the kids. I remember the first time I ever saw the act, when I
was only twelve, I really believed that some crazy farmer stole
an airplane and flew away with it. I swallowed the whole
thing, and so does about sixty or seventy per cent of the audience at my shows — at the outset, anyway. From the beginning of the show, Stanley makes a real pain in the neck of
himself as this farmer who wants a ride in an airplane. Once,
a policeman was so badly fooled he wanted to arrest Stanley,
and we had to do some fast explaining. It takes a lot of stage-
setting by Stanley and me to build up the suspense. Of course,
before too long they all know he's really one hell of a pilot.
He better be. In the farmer act, he's almost always flying on
the edge of a stall. He gets that sucker flying sideways, diving,
looping, standing on its tail — doing everything but spitting
nickels. It's one of the hardest acts in the business, but Stanley makes it look simple. And remember, his airplane is just a
stock Super Cub. He's probably the greatest Cub pilot ever —
and one hell of a nice guy."

Since becoming acquainted with the Segallas, I had heard
several similar tributes to Stanley and his talents from his
colleagues. In fact, the harshest criticism I heard was "He's
always talking a blue streak" — an observation immediately
followed by "But he talks good, doesn't he?" He does. Stanley
Segalla is almost as famous for his non-stop anecdotes as he is
for his practically non-stop aviating. The funny thing is that
he talks like a farmer, with a clipped, rough twang straight out
of rural Connecticut. His weathered, tanned face, topped by a
redneck cap, complements the bucolic image. Only his pene-
trating brown Italian eyes, his dark mustache and sideburns,
and his trim, muscular frame give him the dash of an intrepid
aerobat.

Stanley didn't come by his aviation skills in the military, or out of family tradition. He more or less stumbled into flying. I asked him recently to tell me the story of his life, and he immediately did just that. "I was born right here in Canaan, on December 9, 1924," he said, in what I've come to think of as his Gatling-gun conversational style. "My father, he was named Achille, he came to America when he was fifteen, from a small town near Venice. You see, his brother Giovanni — or John, which is my middle name, because I'm named after him — he came first and was a logger in Canaan. Uncle John made charcoal for the iron furnaces in the area. Later, he was a farmer. My father worked for Uncle John, and then he met my mother, Jennie, who was born in Canaan. She worked in the De Barbieri grocery store. They had ten children — five boys and five girls. Three of the boys died young, of muscular dystrophy, and I'm the older of the living boys — the third oldest of all the children. When I was in school, I worked on the farm for Uncle John, too — from six in the morning till school began, at eight, and then afterward till six at night. I always knew how to work hard.

"My schooling stopped in 1941, when I quit high school to join the Army. I was sixteen, and I spent four years in the Fifth Infantry Division, mostly as a mechanic. Saw some action around Halle, there, in Germany, but then I twisted my spine and was six months in a hospital until I was discharged, in 1945. That's about when I met Ann — Finnegan was her maiden name, and she came from Lee, Massachusetts — and we were married in 1946. Now we have three boys, two girls, and seven grandchildren. All in all, there are at least a hundred of us Segallas in Canaan — Republicans, Democrats, tradesmen, constables (which I was for twenty-four years) — and, with all these Segallas, they never even named a street after us. Anyway, back then, when I was just married, I had to work somewhere, so I got a job as a union carpenter, putting in a new kitchen at The Hotchkiss School, over there in Lakeville. I was paid one dollar and eighty-seven and a half cents an hour, but I guess the dollar went farther then. We got by. I remember there was an ex-B-17 pilot that was my assistant.

"After two years of being a carpenter, I started my own business, mowing lawns and fixing up mowers. My wife helped out. I had five cemeteries to mow, under contract. From five till eight in the morning, I'd repair mowers, then I'd mow, and from six to eleven at night I'd repair some more. In winter, we'd plow snow. Built my own house by myself for six thousand dollars on my father's Canaan property, and added rooms for the kids as they came along. You see, I had this mechanical aptitude, I guess you'd call it. I could always fix anything and make it work good. Loved to tinker. Always did."

Stanley paused to catch his breath, and I asked him how he got into flying airplanes.

"The funny thing was, all that time I had no interest in flying," he answered. "But in 1950 I started getting interested in model airplanes as a hobby — you know, building them from kits, fixing up the engines. I flew them with something called U-Control, which gives you the feel of really flying an airplane. I liked that, but it was as far as my flying, so-called, went, since I didn't have any spare cash for bigger things. Then, one day, I got to talking with a man named Roger Newkirk. He was an undertaker in Canaan and also the president of one of those cemeteries I did mowing for. Mr. Newkirk had bought himself a Taylorcraft, with a sixty-five-horsepower Continental engine, and then he took flying lessons from an instructor up in Great Barrington, just north of Canaan. He got his private license, but he decided that he wanted more of an airplane, so he asked me if I wanted to buy the Taylorcraft for seven hundred dollars. I sure wanted to, but where was I going to get seven hundred dollars? Mr. Newkirk said he'd take a hundred a month out of my cemetery-mowing pay, like an installment plan, and that's how I became the owner of a Taylorcraft in Great Barrington. But I still had to learn to fly the damned thing. That turned out to be easy, thanks to my U-Control practice with the models. I paid an instructor for only four hours of dual time, and then I soloed. After forty hours, I got my private license, and I haven't stopped flying since."

But what did his wife, Ann, have to say about an airplane coming into the family?

"Well, she didn't approve at all," Stanley said. "Not that there was much she could do about it. I just came home and told her we owned an airplane. She went on weekend trips with me — to Martha's Vineyard and places like that — but she never really caught the bug. Later on, she refused to fly at all. 'One of us has to be around for the kids,' she said."

From the first, Stanley was what is known in aviation circles as "a natural pilot." His mechanical aptitude, combined with remarkable depth perception ("I amazed them when they gave me that depth-perception test in the Army") and total fearlessness of flying, helped him to become a master of his new calling. He has logged more than thirteen thousand hours of flying time, and over the years, as he has prospered in his construction business, he has owned a total of thirty-three single-engine airplanes. "My greatest buy was an old Howard DGA-17," he said, "which was a low-wing monoplane with plywood wings, two open cockpits, and a hundred-and-twenty-five-horsepower Kinner engine. I bought it from a guy in East Greenbush, New York, up there near Albany, for seventy-five dollars. Seventy-five dollars! He wanted eighty-five, but I told him I needed ten dollars for gas to fly it home. Only three cylinders were working on that flight home, but I made it. Nice airplane. I also bought a J-3 Cub once, for two hundred and sixty-five. Now, there was a deal!"

As Stanley amassed aircraft, he found he needed a convenient place to put them. Typically, he just went ahead and built his own small grass airfields — first, an eleven-hundred-foot strip on his cousin Fred's land in Canaan, and, later, a twenty-eight-hundred-foot strip on rented land in North Canaan. In 1970, Stanley and five other light-aircraft enthusiasts bought that North Canaan land, enlarging the grass runway to thirty-one hundred feet and constructing a bona-fide, if ramshackle, private airport, complete with small hangars and an operations building. Stanley and his partners base their fleet of light airplanes there and allow the Nutmeg Soaring Association to use it for its gliders and tow planes.

With his own landing strip, several aircraft, and a compulsion to fly in new, daring ways, Stanley drifted into aerobatics. "When I began flying, it was definitely not in the back of my mind to do aerobatics," he said. "What happened was, I was up there one day in my clipped-wing Cub and I started playing around. Before I knew it, I was doing a loop. Then I was doing a roll, and suddenly I was an aerobatic pilot. I never had so much as one hour of aerobatic instruction. I learned by reading about it in a book and going up and trying out what I read. It's a hell of a way to learn, I'll admit, but it worked. The margin for error is not as small as it seems, if you got the stuff, the right airplane, and you're careful. For me, it was like a guy with a good boat, who goes out farther and farther to sea, as a kind of challenge to himself. Of course, that's not true of every pilot — most are satisfied with what they're doing, just flying regular. But I was never really satisfied unless I could keep on doing something different, testing myself and my airplane to see what we could both take before getting torn apart. Just going on a cross-country hop was sort of boring. It's the same with my son Billy."

Billy — who is a youthful mirror image of his father, with a more sensitive face and longer hair — was already flying, so to speak, when most kids are learning to walk. He began his aviation career at the startling age of three and a half years, when Stanley constructed for his son's amusement an airplanelike contraption out of two-by-fours, stretched Irish linen, and a Clinton lawnmower engine with a tiny, homemade propeller. With Billy at the simple controls, the thing rose a mighty eight inches off the ground. (In a weak moment, Stanley later sold the machine. All he has left to remind him of Billy's marvelous toy is a faded, dog-eared photograph.) Billy soloed, illegally, at the age of ten. "I had a couple of pillows under me, and I just took Dad's Super Cub up alone one day," he told me. "I already had an unlogged — because I was underage — three hundred hours of dual instruction by then, so I knew what I was doing. On my sixteenth birthday, I soloed legally, and did some aerobatics. We sent that statistic off to the *Guinness Book of World Records* people, and we're hoping they'll print it as the youngest-aerobatic-pilot entry."

After graduating from the Housatonic Valley Regional High School, in 1978, Billy thought about trying for an appointment to the United States Air Force Academy. Instead, he attended Southern Connecticut State College, in New Haven, for a year, dropped out, and joined his father in both the construction business and the aerobatics business. He performs a solo act at air shows in his fully aerobatic Pitts Special S-1S and teams up with two other pilots, Pete Esposito and Russ Gage, for a triple-plane exhibition. Besides his commercial-pilot's certificate, he has earned a Federal Aviation Administration Statement of Competency that permits him to execute aerobatic maneuvers down to ground level. Billy has gained a growing reputation for his skills, and one day he would like to enter the major aerobatic competitions.

"Maybe it's crazy," Billy said to me, "but you either love doing aerobatics or you don't. Dad took me up in the Cub when I was a little kid and did loops and spins without first

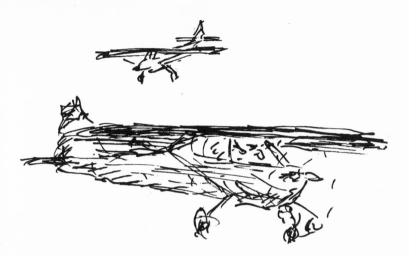

telling me what he was going to do. I loved it. He showed me how, and I just did it. I got more and more into it. I never had doubts or fears. If I did, it would be time to quit. My mother doesn't like it, of course, and my wife, Tammie, doesn't much like it, either — although she's done some aerobatic flying with me. But they'll never try to stop me, because they know I love it so."

THE current Federal Aviation Regulations define aerobatic flight as "an intentional maneuver involving an abrupt change in an aircraft's attitude, an abnormal attitude, or abnormal acceleration, not necessary for normal flight." By "abnormal attitude," the regulations mean a bank of sixty degrees or more, or a pitch angle (climb or dive) of thirty degrees or more. Given these definitions, to say that the Segallas aviate in an almost constant state of aerobatic flight is to say that a yogi stands on his head. At practice sessions and air shows, Billy — either solo or with one or both of the members of his team — performs the following extremely abnormal, and breathtaking, maneuvers:

A double snap roll during takeoff, at a hundred and thirty miles per hour, with smoke trailing from the exhaust. (The smoke is produced by a substance called Corvus oil, which is injected into a hot exhaust pipe.) The snap roll is, in effect, a rapid horizontal spin, in which the airplane revolves about its longitudinal axis while in a high-speed stall.

Inside loops, sometimes punctuated with a snap roll or two at the top of the arc.

Spins, at different velocities and in different dimensions, the number of revolutions precisely controlled.

Various forms of the slow roll and the barrel roll, inside and out.

Vertical rolls, as many as three in a row.

Sustained inverted flight.

Full "hesitation" rolls, in which the airplane halts for a second at various points during the roll: at each forty-five-degree mark in an eight-point hesitation roll; at each ninety-degree mark in a four-point version.

Knife-edge flight — a ninety-degree bank, occasionally culminating, almost at ground level, in the low wing's cutting a ribbon strung between two stanchions.

Square loops, the oxymorons of the repertoire, wherein the loop circle is squared.

Outside loops, during which the negative-G forces hold the blood in the brain, and which often cause the pilot to see red, literally. Billy once did ten consecutive outside loops during a practice session over Canaan.

Mock games of "chicken," in which Billy and one of his teammates streak toward each other at an altitude of about fifty feet on what appears to be a certain collision course. At the last second, each snap-rolls to his right, trailing Corvus-oil smoke.

Cuban Eights, the airplane looping horizontal figure eights, each loop ending at the waist of the eight with a half roll. An aviator named Len Povey improvised this maneuver during a 1936 Miami air show, while he was employed by Fulgencio Batista's government to train Cuban Air Force pilots — hence its name.

Tail slides, or whip stalls, in which the vertical is held until the airplane can no longer climb, whereupon it stalls, backs down on its tail, and finally whips over into a dive. Billy does an even more frightening version of this, called the torque roll: the airplane spins backward for a while, on its tail, before nosing over.

Hammerheads, or vertical climbs capped at the stalling point by a quick, pivoting turn that propels the airplane down the same path it took up.

And the *lomcovák* (a Czech word meaning "uncontrolled gyration"), which is perhaps the most stressful and dangerous of aerobatic tricks. Created by the ever-inventive Czechoslovakians, the *lomcovák* is a high-speed stall followed by an outside snap roll. The airplane then tumbles freely, twisting tail over propeller before plummeting into a vertical dive.

These maneuvers — which Stanley, in his day, also mastered, and several of which he still performs on occasion — must be executed within what aerobats call a "box"; that is, an ideal, prescribed zone of airspace, the length and width being not more than two thousand by four thousand feet for the most powerful aircraft. And to add to the degree of difficulty the lines must be straight, the curves symmetrical, and all the maneuvers harmonious and rhythmic. The tremendous concentration, despite sometimes total disorientation, and the attendant physical punishment make a fifteen-minute aerobatic routine the equivalent of playing an entire football game non-stop. In a sense, it is the most athletic of sports.

This intense strain was made abundantly clear to me not

only while I was watching the Segallas do their routines in air shows but also, oddly enough, one summer evening in Stanley's living room, at his pleasantly casual house in Canaan. His living room — unmistakably the quarters of a dedicated pilot, with its photographs, paintings, and mobiles of airplanes — features Stanley's latest toy: a video camera and recorder, which he uses to review the Segallas' air-show acts. With Stanley, his wife, their daughter Debra, and Billy huddled with me in front of the television set, I had the opportunity to see what was really going on and hear them talk about it at the same time. The videotape Stanley chose was of a recent air show in Pittsfield, Massachusetts.

"I get a kick out of watching these tapes," Stanley said as the screen lit up with a sharp color shot of Billy's spiffy red-and-white Pitts Special biplane. "They have a practical use, too, because we can see where we made our errors and correct ourselves for the next time. And they're good advertisements. I take them down to stag parties and the Rotary — all those guys will want to come to see the shows, maybe. When Billy was first learning aerobatics, I sometimes used to talk to him on a little power-pack radio, and if he was shooting an outside loop or something, I'd tell him he's up on it or he's getting too low, or some other advice. One day, he was practicing over Canaan, and I was on the power-pack radio with him. I see his engine quit, so I tell him to let it out and coast back to the airport and make a dead-stick landing. After he landed, we found that some wasps had built a nest in the air-intake for the fuel vent, and it had made a vacuum in the tank. No air could get in, because of those damn wasps. You never know. When Billy's flying in a routine with Pete and Russ, they talk to each other on the 123.40 frequency, which few other pilots use."

"Pete does most of the talking," Billy added. "He usually yells 'Now!' when he wants us to break."

"And they have diagrams of the routines taped in front of them in their cockpits," Stanley said, "so they don't get confused."

Stanley stopped talking as the video camera followed Billy through the start of his solo. The oohs and ahs of the crowd were echoed by Ann and Debra, who intermittently covered their eyes with their hands as the hundred-and-eighty-horsepower Pitts careered through the verticals, hammerheads, rolls, spins, and loops. "Now, there is where you get a gray-out," Billy said as his airplane curved impossibly upward to an inverted position. "That's from the positive-G forces. It's really more of a brownish-gray. At the top of a regular loop, there's little G force, so you're almost weightless, like an astronaut. Here comes an outside loop, where you get the negative Gs — and a red-out, if you do a lot of them."

"Way up, Billy, get over there!" Stanley shouted at the screen. The Pitts nosed over into a screaming dive, coming in low, hard, and inverted. "You're pushing it in for a tight one," Stanley went on. "OK, push it in, push it in more." With smoke trailing, Billy completed a perfect circle. "OK, beautiful, beautiful. Lovely."

On the tape, the voice of Alan Loncto could be heard over the public-address system saying, "There go the eyeballs into the attic." Ann Segalla left the room.

"It's not as bad as all that," Billy said.

"Now, here's the torque roll," Stanley said. "In 1972, Charlie Hillard won the Men's World Aerobatic Championship with that maneuver. Nobody ever did it in a big competition before. What you do is go straight up, rolling, so that the airplane can't fly forward anymore, and the airplane is just sitting there, the torque of the engine turning it on its tail. You got to hold it steady and balance it while it spins backward. Sometimes it will back down six or seven lengths of the airplane before it noses over into a dive and you can recover." Just as

Stanley described the maneuver, Billy performed it. "He's coming back, he's coming back," Stanley said. "Jesus Christ, he almost blew it! You can stop an engine that way, Billy. When you're coming back hard like that and it quits, the prop can start windmilling the wrong way and you get into a lot of trouble. Then you have to gain speed and start windmilling the right way to re-start the engine." It didn't happen. Billy rolled out at a hundred feet or so above the ground and wagged his wings at the crowd. "Billy's good," Stanley said, with a curt nod. Billy smiled.

"As I say," Stanley continued, "that Charlie Hillard invented the torque roll, and you got to wonder about the first time he ever did it. Really something to do a maneuver like that for the first time ever. Like the *lomcovák*, which is coming up next. The Czech guy who did that first, he almost tore the airplane apart. Now, watch Billy do it. See, he brings the airplane up at about a hundred and twenty miles per hour, and it loses all its lift — can't fly anymore. He kicks it into an outside snap roll, pushes the stick forward, and the airplane doesn't know what the hell to do. It wants to go this way and that, tumbling around end over end. That's the *lomcovák* for you. You have to wait until it stops tumbling and start it up from there. Damn, he just went into a spin afterward, but he's OK. It never comes out the same way."

Billy studied his recovery from the *lomcovák* critically, then shrugged, as if to say, What the hell, I made it, didn't I? "I learned how to do the *lomcovák* by reading about it," he said, "and then I tried it myself. Now I do it all the time. The harder maneuvers, like that one, with more stress on the airplane — you have to think about them a lot before you try them. And about how to get out of them, too. For instance, you can't get out of a torque roll until the nose drops. Then you start your recovery."

After the grand *lomcovák* finale, Billy's Pitts slipped in for a landing, and the crowd cheered. "Hey, Billy, way to go!" somebody yelled, and Billy waved from his cockpit in appreciation, the sun glinting off his dark glasses. The Segallas, father and son, stared at the screen looking pleased, and Ann returned to the living room.

While other events at the Pittsfield air show — demonstrations by Air National Guard jets, helicopters, parachutists, refurbished Second World War "warbirds" — flitted back and forth on the screen, I chatted with the Segalla family about the rigors of aerobatics. What about eating? Is there a special diet for aerobats before a performance?

Billy answered first. "No problem," he said. "I eat anything. I got my father's stomach."

To which his father added, "Well, like tonight, for instance. I come home from work, eat a big supper, and fifteen minutes later I feel like doing some flying. I drive over to my airport and take up my Decathlon 8KCAB, which is rated fully aerobatic, and do some outside loops and everything else. Doesn't bother me at all. Once, though, I ate a grinder just before I had to do an air show. Flying over to the show, I could feel that grinder right there in my gut — burning a hole, you know? I had to do something, so I made three or four loops right in a row, and whatever was bothering me got pushed down, and I was cured, just like that. Fixed me right up."

And what about the crowds that attend the shows? Alan Loncto had told me that the sad part of his business was the element in the air-show audience that came out to see blood, to witness somebody getting killed. As Loncto put it, "they think, Hey, maybe we'll see a crash today!"

Stanley said that he doesn't worry about those people. "I like the real fans," he said. "The people who travel all over to see our shows and appreciate what we're doing. Of course, accidents do happen. I've had a few, I guess — some forced landings, a collision. Once, at Rhinebeck, I was doing the

Flying Farmer Act with a new ending, where I would shut off the Cub's engine at two thousand feet, dive at about a hundred and twenty miles per hour, and then do a dead-stick loop, coming out of it at sixteen hundred feet, going into a spin, leveling off at a thousand, and making a dead-stick landing. Anyway, some bad weather came in. I hit a downdraft and went into a flat-out spin with no engine. I recovered, finally, but I was below the tree line. I spotted a hayfield and came in under some telephone wires. I landed dead-stick and in one piece. Meanwhile, everybody had seen me headed for a sure crash, and the fire trucks and the ambulance were on the way. I just got out of the cockpit and hand-started the prop — the Cub has no self-starter, you know — and I took right off from that hayfield. I proceeded to finish the act in the usual way, making a dead-stick landing on the runway just when the fire trucks and the ambulance arrived at the hayfield. The announcer made like it was all part of the act, but it sure wasn't. When somebody congratulated me on the greatest stunt he'd ever seen, I said, 'And that's the last time you'll ever see it.' "

Ann looked as if she wanted to leave the room again. I asked Stanley and Billy if they thought that they were born to fly the way they do.

Billy said, "I don't believe that flying is in the genes; otherwise, my brothers and sisters would be fliers, too. Like Debbie, here."

Debra, who owns and runs Deb's Deli, in Canaan, said that she had once wanted to fly but had lost interest after she got her driver's license. "Why be up there when I can be having as much fun down here?" she said.

"I started flying late in life," Stanley said. "You can't exactly say I was born in the back seat of an airplane. But if you have the ability and you get those basics down pat, then it's a matter of pride, of teaching yourself to be better and better. To be a natural, though, you got to have that seat-of-the-pants type of thing — the special feel for what you're doing. The really good aerobatic pilots are seat-of-the-pants pilots. The nuts, the so-called stunt fliers — they're the ones who don't last in the business very long."

"If somebody calls us stunt fliers, we get kind of angry," Billy added. "We're precision aerobatic pilots — technicians. We follow guidelines set by the FAA, and we have careful briefings before the shows. We don't push our capabilities. But the stunt fliers out in the desert, where nobody is supposed to be — they'll go off and do their things, like crashing up old airplanes that you wouldn't even want to sit in on the ground, wing walking, flying through barns, and everything like that. Then they just patch up the airplanes and fly some more. Of course, some of them, like Art Scholl, fly for the movies and TV, and they're really good aerobatic pilots, too. But mostly it's show business."

"They even have a stunt where a Cub lands on what's called the world's smallest airport," Stanley said, "which is a car with three little pads on its roof. It drives up the runway, and a guy flies his Cub at the same speed as the car, puts his two main wheels down on two of the pads, then settles his tail wheel on the third pad, and the car drives off the runway. I got to admit that's a damn good trick."

Billy rose to leave, saying he had to get home to his wife. His father saw him to the door, and they exchanged some technical talk about their next show. When Stanley returned to the living room, he said to me, "Billy is a great pilot and a great kid. I boss him around a lot, and yell at him too much sometimes, but he's the best. Doesn't smoke or drink, and he's real serious about his flying. He could be an international champion, like that Charlie Hillard. He's got what it takes, but he needs a sponsor. It's a full-time job, going to competitions, and there's very little pay. The money he earns from his shows now just about pays for the gas, the insurance, and other expenses. But he's young, and he's got a good career ahead of him. I guess I'm reliving my youth through him. Meanwhile, I'll just keep plugging along — flying until I can't pass the physical, and then I'll have to quit."

I asked Ann how she felt about that.

"I'll be happy when the end of October comes and the air-show season finishes," she said. Calliope music sounded from the television set, signaling the start of the Flying Farmer Act. Stanley, with a satisfied chuckle, settled back to watch himself perform his specialty.

FOR many years now, Stanley has been perfecting his version of the Flying Farmer Act, primarily at the Old Rhinebeck

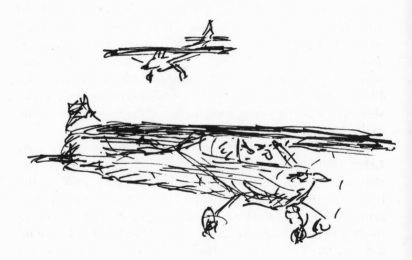

Aerodrome on spring, summer, and fall Sundays. It is at Rhinebeck that he truly flowers, among familiar, intimate surroundings, and it was in this natural habitat that I wanted to see his definitive performance. The Old Rhinebeck Aerodrome — the "Museum in the Sky," as it is billed — sprang from the vision of Cole Palen, a veteran pilot and collector of antique aircraft. Needing a home base for his growing inventory of antiques, Palen bought a dilapidated Rhinebeck farm in 1958, built hangars for his airplanes, and later enlisted pilots with similar interests, like Stanley, to fly the ancient crates for a paying audience and to conduct scenic rides in a rattly biplane for the more courageous tourists. It was all in the old barnstorming tradition, but with a big difference: the crowd was not only entertained but taught something about early aviation. The aerodrome contains a hangar-museum full of aviatorial relics, and the Sunday air show features a narrated playlet concerning First World War characters and aircraft. Over the years, Stanley has flown most of the old airplanes used in the Great War scenario, and he has starred in the shooting down of the "Black Baron" at the end of the show, dogfighting in a reconstructed 1915 Avro 504-K biplane, which is powered by an old hundred-and-ten-horsepower Le Rhône rotary engine. His Flying Farmer Act was added to the show in 1964, and now he generally leaves the antique flying to the younger pilots.

On a still, steamy summer morning, the Sunday of the 1983 Labor Day weekend, I met Stanley at his North Canaan airstrip in order to fly with him in his PA-11 Super Cub the twenty-eight miles to the Old Rhinebeck Aerodrome. When I arrived, the airstrip was already stirring, with glider pilots of the Nutmeg Soaring Association preparing their sleek craft for a day of hunting and riding thermals. Stanley drove up in his 1974 red Cadillac (rear plate, STUNT-1; front plate, I'D RATHER BE FLYING). He was wearing khaki coveralls adorned with bright patch emblems ("International Aerobatic Club," "Experimental Aircraft Association"), a red-and-white redneck cap, white-and-black sneakers, and sunglasses. In a supermarket paper bag he toted his act costume: a farmer's straw hat, ragged denim jeans and jacket, and a red bandanna. Also in the bag was a length of rope to which were fastened several tattered pieces of apparel. "This is a new thing I'm putting into the act," Stanley announced proudly. "I call it Mrs. Finnegan's clothesline — Finnegan is my wife's maiden name, you know — and the idea is I tie one end of it to the Cub and let the rest fly out behind the airplane, so it looks like I picked up Mrs. Finnegan's wash that's been hanging out to dry when I go low behind the trees. Then the announcer can say 'Hey, you got Mrs. Finnegan's wash there!' or something like that." He seemed as pleased as a kid waiting to try out a dribble glass on his unsuspecting parents. (Stanley often adds new props to his routine. At a later air show, he installed an electronic musical horn on the Cub which, at the push of a button, played such tunes as the "Marche Funèbre," "Take Me Out to the Ballgame," "In My Merry Oldsmobile," the "William Tell" Overture, and the Ohio State fight song. Since the engine noise makes the tunes all but unidentifiable, the horn is really for his own amusement.)

Together, we preflighted both the Super Cub, for the Rhinebeck show, and the Decathlon, which Stanley had agreed to fly in a free-lance aerobatic display over the fairgrounds at Goshen, Connecticut, later that afternoon. He was full of beans, talking constantly while doing the pre-flight chores. "I like to keep my airplanes topped off with oil when I'm doing aerobatics," he said, pouring oil from a plastic bottle into the Cub's engine. "And I carry only about five gallons of gas in the tank — just enough to get to Rhinebeck, do my act, and get back. I want it light. Those cables on the tail I check carefully. If they're loose, I'm in trouble. Everything else seem OK? Well, let's roll her out and go. You climb in and crack the throttle, and I'll hand-prop it. You remember how the Cub works?"

I said I did; I had learned to fly, when I was a teen-ager, in a less powerful model of the Super Cub — the Piper J-3.

While I buckled myself into the rear seat, with its dual controls, Stanley stowed his paper bag and oil bottle, primed the engine, made a few adjustments, and told me about a passenger who claimed he knew about Cubs but opened the throttle to full while Stanley spun the prop. On that occasion, the airplane instantly roared to a breakneck taxi speed, just missing Stanley, and circled wildly around the airstrip before the fellow thought to cut the engine. "I learned from that not to trust most people in Cubs," Stanley said.

N4568M, the tiny yellow taildragger that Stanley calls his office, is your basic airplane. It was manufactured in 1946 — one of the first of the Super Cubs. Since 1965, when Stanley acquired it for fifteen hundred dollars, he has installed three new engines, and he has chalked up more than twenty-two hundred flying hours in it. Its instrument panel holds only the bare essentials for a plausible airplane: airspeed indicator, tachometer, turn-and-bank indicator, altimeter, vertical-velocity indicator, oil-temperature and oil-pressure gauges, and fuel gauge — and, solely for Stanley's spiritual benefit, an artificial rose and an adhesive placard bearing the legend "THINK." No radio. No navigational devices, except a magnetic compass. The joystick, the rudder and heel-brake pedals, the magneto switch, the primer, the carburetor-heat knob, the elevator trimmer, and a cable for igniting a smoke bomb round out his office equipment. Once the engine turns over, it is a very noisy office indeed.

Taxiing to the south end of the grass runway, Stanley waved to the glider pilots and kept up his usual patter, the louder patter of the engine notwithstanding. He was as casual and comfortable in his Cub as, say, an old-hand New York City cabbie is with his trusty Checker — talking and gesticulating but always in complete mastery over the machine, which seems to be merely an extension of himself. We took off effortlessly into the hazy north, turned left over the narrow, muddy Housatonic River and the pinewoods and scrub that bound the airstrip, and set a magnetic heading of 270 for Rhinebeck. "Keep an eye out for those gliders!" Stanley shouted over his left shoulder. "They're always where you least expect them. See — there's one two hundred feet above us to the left." We climbed watchfully to twelve hundred feet. "I guess I know this route pretty well after nineteen years," he said. "Once, when the weather and visibility were real bad, I flew just fifty feet above the roads in order to navigate to Rhinebeck."

Every estate, farm, and physical landmark we flew over elicited a story. When Stanley spotted some hikers on a ridge along the Appalachian Trail, he couldn't resist circling them, rocking his wings and waving. The hikers waved back and yelled something. Stanley opened the Cub's double doors in an attempt to make out what they were saying. He banked steeply, then leaned out and shouted, "Hey, louder! Can't hear you! I bet you'll remember this more than your hike!"

We cruised over the treeless pastureland of Dutchess County at ninety-five miles per hour, and Stanley said that his engine sounded good. "When I do a loop in this Cub, I get it up to a hundred and ten," he said. "That way, if the engine decides to quit I still have plenty of speed to make it over the top."

I asked him if he had ever participated in a loop marathon.

"No," he said, "but once I did sixty-four spins at an air show in Vermont, and the announcer counted them off over the P.A. as I did them. I started at eight thousand feet and kept spinning real slow till I got down to one thousand. Sixty-four spins in seven thousand feet. I could've done some more, but I didn't trust my altimeter. Pretty good, though, huh? . . . You see that country club down there, near the Taconic Parkway? That's owned by the guy who sells all that ice cream — Carvel, Tom Carvel. Well, a couple of years ago I did an air show for him over there, and afterward I landed on one of his greens. This old Tom Carvel, he comes over to me and says, 'What's the matter, you're not going to give me a ride?' So I say, 'Sure I will,' and so we go up together. Then he says, 'Aren't you going to do any loops?,' and so I do a loop. He's getting on toward eighty, you know . . . Now just ahead is the Rhinebeck Aerodrome."

I could make out what looked like a movie set for a First World War film — façades representing French and German buildings, vintage aircraft parked along a turf strip, various old cars and trucks darting about. Stanley flew across the field at about a thousand feet, rocked his wings, and pulled up sharply into a stall, which he twisted into a one-and-a-half-turn spin. We lost altitude fast before leveling out into a final approach for landing.

"Was all that to let them know it's you?" I asked.

"Oh, they know it's me, all right," Stanley said.

He landed easily, on the first tenth of the twenty-two-hundred-foot runway, and taxied, with his tail up, to a parking spot at the other end, as nonchalantly as a man pulling into his own driveway. It was only ten o'clock, but the heat and humidity were strong on the field. Stanley sniffed the air and looked around. "They should get three thousand people today," he said. "At five dollars a head for adults and two dollars per kid, that's not bad. Me, I'll get my usual paycheck for the farmer act, which should cover my expenses and time. You don't get rich doing aerobatics. That's why I got a good contracting business, thank God." He greeted his friends and colleagues, many of whom were already in their costumes for the Great War playlet — German, French, and British uniforms, with appropriate mustaches, headgear, and leather boots — and then sauntered toward the office across the field. "I got to pick up my smoke bomb for the act," he told me, "and I'll show you around the museum and the hangars. Then I'm going to take a little rest. The show doesn't begin till two-thirty, and I want to rest up, because I have that other show over Goshen later on."

He enjoyed precious little rest, however. Showing me the museum inspired him to ever-fuller explanations, laced with loving anecdotes, about every aviation curiosity on display. "See that Spartan C-3? Found it over in Northampton, falling apart in a hangar. The guy only wanted five thousand. A nice workhorse. Fixed up, it runs beautiful. You could do aerobatics all day in that. . . . Now, this American Eagle — I was going to buy it for eighteen hundred. Everyone talked me out of it. Today, it's probably worth eighty thousand." Some of the airplanes were once used in the movie *Those Magnificent Men in Their Flying Machines,* and they still look eminently flyable. "That Cole Palen, he owns all this," Stanley said, with a sweep of his arm. "Me and the other pilots, we were just playing around for the fun of it. Of course, we didn't know what Rhinebeck would wind up as one day." While conducting me through the nearby hangars, where the aircraft are worked on by four full-time mechanics, Stanley came upon his old Avro 504-K, which he used to fly in "combat" against the Black Baron during the war skit's climax. The biplane, with British markings, was in for serious engine repairs. Stanley patted its tail affectionately. "More of these were built in the First World War than any other airplane," he said. "With the Avro rotary engine, it's either full throttle or off. Tricky to fly, but fun. I used that one-shot gun mounted on the front to shoot down the Black Baron. Only one shot, so you had to make it good. They billed me as One-Shot Gatling in the program. No more of that stuff for me, though."

Two hours passed quickly and delightfully on the guided tour. After we had lunch — cheeseburgers, French fries, and Cokes at a refreshment stand — Stanley told Robert Tholl, the P.A. narrator, about Mrs. Finnegan's clothesline. Tholl approved the latest addition to the act with an indulgent smile. "It won't get fouled up in the tail, will it?" he asked.

"Naw," Stanley answered. "I'll just let it hang out behind, and then I'll fly across with my leg sticking out the door, same as I always do, and the clothes trailing. You say something like 'Oh-oh, he's got Mrs. Finnegan's clothesline, and she'll be coming after him.' I remember Bob Weymouth, out of Maine — he used to do the clothesline thing in *his* farmer act. Weymouth's an old guy, about sixty — well, about my age, I guess. But I don't think there's anybody except me who does the farmer act and shuts the engine off at the end and makes a dead-stick landing. I've seen a lot of them, but nobody's ever done it yet like me."

"They're all smarter, that's why," Tholl said, to general laughter. "By the way, Stanley, I wish you'd remember to yell 'Help!' when you're up there."

"I do holler," Stanley said.

"We can't hear you. Holler louder."

At last, Stanley walked over to the office for his postponed rest, stopping to gab with just a few other pilots. I wandered about, absorbing the atmosphere as the performers checked their equipment and the audience filed in. A green-and-yellow 1929 New Standard D-25 biplane was in constant use, flying four passengers at a time on fifteen-minute rides over the Hudson River and back. The non-flying customers flocked to the souvenir shop (stocked with such items as helmets with goggles, T-shirts, and posters), the refreshment booths, and the shadier bleacher seats. Ragtime and 1917 patriotic music blared from the public-address system. Pilots tested their oxyacetylene-fired "machine guns" and their raucous engines along the infield. A German armored car (actually, a Maxwell covered with plywood), a 1917 olive-drab Model T marked "US 22nd Aero Sqd," an authentic American Expeditionary Force ambulance, and old cars and motorcycles buzzed fitfully into position in front of façades with signs reading "DER SAUSAGE FACTORY UND GAZWERKS," "FIFI," "HOTEL DE PAREE," "DER BADZ BOYZ." It was noisy and fun, like a combination movie and carnival. I wondered if Stanley was getting any rest.

Before long, it was time for the pilots' meeting, in the infield pit area. Stanley emerged from the office, looking thoroughly unrested, and joined the other pilots. They gathered around the Model T to listen to Bill Hammond, the chief pilot, summarize the events and perils of the day's program. Hammond, dressed in a German uniform for his role as Whispering Willie, the Happy Heinie, called the assembly to order and said, "There's a new Trudy Truelove today, and a new Madame Fifi, too, so if you can give them some directions for the show I think they'd appreciate it. Dick will do the 'Bombs Bursting in Air,' and there are two of them today, so you guys know the second one is your cue. The first one is the flag. . . . Ribbon cuts are all covered, I guess. . . . The balloon is out of commission. There'll be a four-plane dogfight, so that should be back to normal. . . . Farmer act? All set, Stanley? Incidentally, Stanley is going to leave for the Goshen show during the bombing raid. So, bomber pilots, while you guys are bombing, Stanley will probably scoot out at some point. Don't hit him. The first bombing raid is on the hotel and the last is on the sausage factory. No dive-bombing, please." After a few more advisories, the meeting broke up, with all the joshing and camaraderie of a real mission, and the pilots manned their planes.

Stanley went back to the office to don his farmer's garb. He soon reappeared in character, sipping from a wine bottle (which contained iced tea), weaving tipsily through the crowd, and demanding a free ride from the pilots in "one of them there aeroplanes, before I have to get home to my cows."

What took place thereafter was nothing less than a three-ring aerial circus. The main characters of the Great War playlet were introduced in the manner of a road-company opéra-bouffe troupe, with corny narration, as they indulged in exaggerated screams, shouts, and gestures — all this punctuated by exploding black-powder bombs, shattering flybys, popping machine guns, and daredevil ribbon-cutting stunts. The plot line of the playlet tries one's comprehension. Suffice it to say that the villainous, goose-stepping Black Baron, acted by Cole Palen himself ("Boy, he's a real bad guy," says the narrator, Tholl. "Watch out for him!"), captures the French town, including pretty Trudy Truelove. Mme. Fifi, the owner of a lingerie shop, entreats Pierre de Loop de Loop to rescue her friend Trudy. "Go up in your flying machine and find her," she declaims above the clamor. "I shall find Trudy Truelove for you," Pierre vows, shaking his fist. "For you, *mon amour*, anyzing. *Au revoir*." Much bombing and strafing follow from a balky Morane-Saulnier monoplane piloted by Pierre, who upon landing explains to Fifi, "I miss wiz ze bombs and I blow up your longeray shop." An effigy of Trudy is ultimately dropped into a haystack by a compatriot of the Black Baron; the live Trudy emerges unharmed from the hay; and Sir Percy Goodfellow, a British ace, is in turn captured.

The audience, bemused as I, loves the flying and the commotion, however. And all through the mishmash, oblivious of the goings on, Farmer Stanley is poking drunkenly about and bothering everybody. From time to time, Tholl reminds the crowd of Stanley's presence: "What's that farmer doing out there on the field? Hey, you! Come back here with the rest of the folks! You're going to get hurt out there!" At last, the Fifi-Pierre-Trudy-Percy-Black Baron action subsides to a dull clatter, and Stanley's little yellow Super Cub is wheeled out to the center of the field. All eyes are on the pushy farmer.

"OK, you'll get your ride now, Mr. Farmer," the narrator says. "Will one of the pilots take him up, please, so we can get on with the show?" Stanley, beaming and waving his straw hat, is belted into the rear seat of the Cub, and a pilot (sometimes played by Billy) seats himself in the front. The propeller is spun by one of the ground crew, the engine sputters to life. But something seems to be wrong with the tail wheel, and the pilot leaves the airplane to correct the alleged problem. Suddenly, with Stanley solo, the Cub roars to full power, turning spastically and scattering the bystanders. Collective gasps and screams. Stanley yells "Hey, let me out!" and then loses his hat.

"What's going on there?" says Tholl. "That fellow can't fly an airplane. Tell him to take his hand off the throttle. Stop him, somebody! Oh no!" And with that, Stanley guns the Cub down part of the runway and — rudder wiggling, on one wheel — bounces into the air, careering erratically to an altitude of fifty feet. A ground-crew member hangs Stanley's straw hat on a stake near the runway. "When he comes back, he won't need a hat," says the narrator.

The Cub goes straight up for a moment and then dips alarmingly behind some trees in front of the bleachers. "Oh no, he's in the trees," moans Tholl. The crowd shrieks, and the Instamatics start clicking, trying to catch the expected ball of flame, the black cloud of smoke. But there is no flame, no smoke. Instead, there is the Cub, stuttering upward and dragging a clothesline of laundry. The crowd is at once relieved, slightly disappointed, and amused. The joke is on them. "He's got Mrs. O'Reilly's clothesline!" Tholl exclaims, forgetting that it was supposed to be Mrs. Finnegan's clothesline. "She's sure going to be mad! Gee, should we call the State Police?"

The pretense having vanished, Stanley stands the Cub on its tail and climbs to six hundred feet, whereupon he executes brilliant inside loops seriatim, his smoke bomb ignited and trailing white vapor alongside the clothesline. Again he climbs straight up, and this time he stalls and plunges toward the runway, ending in a spin just above the ground. The audience is with him every second, and isn't listening to Tholl, who persists with his ringmaster-to-clown monologue. ("Hey, look out — that's a Piper Cub! You can't do that. You'll pull the wings right off it!") Stanley repeats the maneuver, which is his version of a hammerhead, and then buzzes the field, leaning out of the open double doors and presumably yelling "Help!" He goes vertical once more, stalls the engine, and restarts it by windmilling the propeller. More loops follow, and then, in very slow flight over the field, just above stall speed, he does a full barrel roll, a spin and loop, a half-loop, and inverted flight. He rolls upright, heads back toward the field, and cuts his engine. The propeller makes a few revolutions and stops. "He's had it," says the narrator. "He's out of gas."

He is not out of gas, of course, but his engine is obviously dead, and he is out of landing space. The consuming questions of how and where he's going to land the airplane force an eerie silence. Clown or ace, he's not going to make it. But Stanley dives a bit to gain some speed, veers to his left behind the tree line, and miraculously reappears with just enough altitude to turn and slip into a dead-stick landing, the Cub bumping along the ground right up to the stake holding his straw hat. Without missing a beat, he snatches the hat, places it on his head, and jumps from the airplane to a standing ovation — the just reward for a virtuosic performance.

But it's not over yet. Stanley acknowledges the applause and returns to the Cub. He starts the engine by leaning over the right wing strut and flipping the propeller. He hops inside and, at full throttle, makes the game, forgiving airplane do some ground tricks, like a venerable trained elephant — tail up and turning in dizzying circles on its main gear. Stanley raises his arms, as if to say, "Look, Ma, no hands!" Finally, he parks the airplane. Another ovation.

"There he is, folks — Stanley Segalla, of Canaan, Connecticut," says Tholl. "He's been doing this for seventeen years."

"Nineteen years!" shouts Stanley, from across the field.

"I didn't know you were *that* old," replies the narrator.

As Stanley made his way to the office to change his clothes, he received his public. People of all ages mobbed him, demanding his autograph and asking him to pose for photographs. One young man wanted to trade hats with him, and another asked whether he could take aerobatic lessons at the North Canaan airstrip. Stanley looked tired, but happily tired — like the leading actor in a long-running Broadway hit who wallows in the attention paid him no matter how many times he has played his role. He was unquestionably the star of the show. The Great War skit was grinding toward its grand finale — the bombing raid and the dogfight with the Black Baron — but nobody seemed to care very much. It was all an anticlimax after the Flying Farmer Act.

By three-thirty, Stanley and I were back in the Cub, zooming off the turf while three antique airplanes circled Fifi's lingerie shop dropping black-powder bombs. I sensed that the crowd was watching us instead of the bombers. So did Stanley: for a moment, he joined in the bombing formation, wiggling his tail, getting in the act one last time. Then we flew east, toward Canaan, leaving the ruckus behind — a mad, sur-realistic scene for a summer Sunday afternoon in Dutchess County, New York. As Stanley flew the Cub, his shoulders sagged. For the first time since I'd met him, he had nothing to say. He almost looked his age. I asked him if he wanted me to take the controls for a while so he could relax, and he con-sented. The Cub, for all the abuse it had taken, handled beau-tifully. I slowly climbed to two thousand feet, to clear a ridge ahead, and enjoyed the placid scenery below. To the south, a thick, wet haze was brewing. Ten wordless, exhilarating min-utes passed.

"Looks like some weather coming in," Stanley said, at last. "Hope it doesn't get too bad. I'm supposed to be performing over Goshen at four-thirty. I'll radio the fair director from the Decathlon and try to time my appearance to his announcing, do a few aerobatics, and then head straight home. I can sleep late tomorrow, on Labor Day. . . . Hey, the crowd really liked that clothesline, don't you think? And how about that full roll I did! Nice and smooth. It's not so easy to do in a Cub. You can't put those wings around, they're so big. The secret is to use plenty of rudder."

I complimented him on his scary dead-stick landing at Rhinebeck.

"Yeah," he said. "You got to time it just right, be right on the ball. One of the loops I did there, I knew I didn't have the power to make it over the top, so I shoved the airplane into a spin and picked up enough speed for the engine to catch again. You know, it's the same routine time after time, but something always makes it a little different. I have to admit I love it. I still get as big a kick out of it as the folks do."

He seemed to be pumping up his second wind for the Goshen show. Just being aloft again and talking about aero-batics were reviving him, making him younger. "Hey," he said, "let's do some loops. I'll take the controls, and you follow me through." He advanced the throttle, eased the joystick forward, and, as we dived toward a Connecticut recreational area known as Twin Lakes, pulled back on the stick. The horizon abruptly vanished and was replaced by gray sky. The positive Gs pressed me against the seat and leadened my eyelids and jaw. I felt giddy, gray-brained. For a second, we were inverted, over the top. Stanley increased the back pressure on the stick and reduced the power. We whooshed downward to the same horizon we had just left. He glanced back to see if I was all right. I was; in fact, I was ecstatic.

"Now we'll do a Cuban Eight," Stanley said. Just after the apogee of an inside loop, with the Cub inverted, he half-rolled into a dive, looped once more, again executing a half-roll after the apogee, and dived to the exact point at which we had started. It was all over in about fifteen seconds, but we had changed our course a hundred and eighty degrees twice, without leaving the vertical plane. Amazing and thrilling. For an encore — to, I'm sure, the entertainment of the boaters and swimmers below — Stanley performed another flawless inside loop, and then descended to Canaan. The aerobatic interlude was exquisite, and something only those who experience it can fully appreciate. Beyond the sheer excitement, there is the sense of having accomplished a Promethean act, of having triumphed over natural laws. It is showing off, of course, but it is also something much more profound.

After we landed, Stanley parked the Cub in its shed, wheeled out the Decathlon, checked it over one more time, strapped on his parachute ("I carry a chute for higher-altitude routines," he said. "Down low, like my work in the Cub, you wouldn't have time, or room, to use it"), and revved up the trig red-white-and-blue airplane for the five-minute flight to Goshen. He said goodbye to me, apologizing for the rush, and taxied to the north end of the grass strip. A misty, barely perceptible rain began to fall. The glider pilots were packing it in for the day. I stood on the damp grass and watched the Decathlon, navigation lights flashing, streak down the runway. All eyes were once again on Stanley Segalla. At four hundred feet off the ground, he expelled some Corvus-oil smoke, spun into a snap roll, and climbed steeply to the southeast. Within a few seconds, his blinking lights had disappeared in the soggy haze.

As it became more generally known that I was a pilot (albeit a short-time pilot), a curious pattern took shape. People who had read my pieces on flying wrote letters to me, indicating their own affection for private aviation. Most of the letters were, unsurprisingly, from present or former licensed pilots, but several were from just plain earthbound folks — individuals who had gazed longingly upward at small aircraft and wanted, somehow, someday, to fly one of them. They would movingly confess this strange yearning, and I would answer them by saying, in effect, it's never too late; as long as you have your wits, your health, and some spare cash, you, too, can be a pilot.

At the same time, I noticed that at parties and such I would frequently be buttonholed by acquaintances who questioned me about my hobby-compulsion. Many of them also confessed to the strange yearning. Particularly odd, I found, was their attitude toward private aviation: it was anachronistic, almost as if we were living in, say, the nineteen-twenties. Even in this age of commonplace space shots, supersonic jet travel, and fighter-bombers and missiles that do everything but balance your checkbook, people still talked about light airplanes with the same awe and feeling of adventure that, I imagine, Charles Lindbergh heard (and shrank from) in 1927.

"Can you really trust those little planes?" they would ask.

"How high can you go?"

"What does it feel like up there?"

"Can it really fly on just one engine?"

"What do you do if you run out of gas?"

"Where do you go in them?" And when I told them that I especially like to fly to small airports they probably never heard of, they would ask, "But how can you land at one of those places if there isn't even a control tower or a big paved runway?"

Finally, the sometimes wearisome, repetitive questions (and my wearisome, repetitive answers) prompted me to write about small airports and the people who inhabit them. Once again, the flying and the writing were happily complementary.

AFTER the Second World War, America found itself with thousands of young men and women who had learned to fly airplanes and who wanted to keep on flying, not necessarily as a profession. About the same time, American businessmen discovered aviation as an efficient tool for increasing sales and prestige. And there were those, like me, who were too young to fly in the war but who yearned to control a machine in the sky. As a result of all this, general aviation — that is, civil flying other than scheduled and nonscheduled carriers — flowered throughout the land. Newspaper and magazine feature stories predicted that recreational aircraft would soon be as common to America's middle class as the second car, and for a while it seemed almost possible. War-surplus airplanes and inexpensive new "family" four-seaters were readily available; fuel was cheap; the economic picture was rosy. The elders of cities and towns felt that a municipal airport was as much a necessity for modern existence as, say, a Holiday Inn franchise. These local airports sprouted in the most unlikely places, on any nearby acreage deemed level; and deserted military air bases were converted into civilian roosts for indigenous fliers. They were emblems of progress and development.

Some small airfields began as just privately owned grass strips in a farmer's back forty, where a personal airplane and those of a few friends might be quartered. Such "farmer fields," as they were called, often grew into something more substantial, with real hangars, full-time mechanics, flight schools, charter services, coffee shops, and control towers. Most, however, never quite made it past the grass-strip stage. Indeed, as the dream of a family airplane for weekend jaunts became more elusive because of rising costs and the increasingly technical nature of flying, the once-solvent airports suffered. In recent years — with aviation-fuel prices five times what they were before 1973, with airplanes and flight lessons double the price, and with stringent federal limitations on light-aircraft flying — many airport owners have sold out to industrial-park and shopping-mall developers. The old saying among airport operators is: "In hard times, aviation goes down the tube first." Still, by and large, the small airport is hanging in there, sometimes little more than an expensive plaything for the determined owner or municipality.

Since I have taken up private flying again, a particular joy for me has been dropping in, literally and figuratively, on several of these tenuous airports around the Northeast. A few of them I had to visit as part of my cross-country training toward my private-pilot's license, but now, when I have no pressing destination in mind, I occasionally hop over to some insignificant field for the sheer fun of it. Fun it is because you don't have the worries of traffic congestion and rigid control that are attendant on the larger, well-known airports. And the people who run and use the small fields have long struck me as generally a curious lot, sort of the last eccentrics of contemporary high-tech aviation. That's part of the fun, too: chatting with peers who seem to be, well, different from the rest of monolithic America. In the course of my visits to small airports, I've met a computer engineer who abandoned his profitable career so he could tinker all day long with his ancient light airplane; a flying grandmother who has no intention of ever giving up her favorite sport; an airline captain who practically lost his job and his wife in order to construct his home-built aerobatic two-seater; a businessman-aviator who invents spurious business trips so he can enjoy splendid solitude in his Piper Arrow; and a lot of people who are strangely like me. What we all have in common is a pervasive attraction to light aircraft and what they can do for the human spirit. We come in all sizes, shapes, sexes, and backgrounds, but we tend to be cut from the same cloth. As one of our number, a semi-professional flier who would work at any menial task to support his habit, once told me: "We're all like a goddam college fraternity. We may have different prejudices and strong political feelings — usually conservative, I think — but that stuff disappears when we meet another member of the frat. He or she is immediately accepted because he or she is a light-airplane pilot. You just know that in most cases the person is self-reliant, an individualist, a first-rater, who knows what he's doing or he probably wouldn't have that little piece of cardboard from the government certifying that he's an airman. Of course, there are plenty of turkeys masquerading as pilots, but almost everybody I've ever met who flies is kind of special — somebody I want to be with."

Not long ago, I was talking to my friend Ed Koren, the artist known for his woolly, barely anthropomorphic subjects, about small airports and their habitués. Ed, who isn't a pilot but is as fascinated by flying as any licensed airman, expressed interest in accompanying me on some trips to see these offbeat people and places. (That I described them as apt studies for his pen didn't dull his interest any.) We agreed to arrange our trips casually, flying when the weather was pleasant and when our schedules were uncrowded. The first trip was to be a trial run — to a little field at Stormville, in Dutchess County, New York, just seventeen nautical miles from my home airport in Danbury, Connecticut.

Friday, October 21, 1983

METEOROLOGICALLY speaking, this day is a winner, a beauty for our maiden voyage. Last night brought the first frost of the season, and the clean, crisp air it left behind has produced the very definition of what pilots call, in their passion for abbreviation and acronym, CAVU — ceiling and visibility unlimited. Severe clear. As the sun rises higher this morning, it is getting agreeably warmer by the minute.

Ed and I have arranged to meet at the Sadler Aero Center, a part of the Danbury Municipal Airport, at ten-thirty, but I arrive at Sadler an hour early to preflight my rented two-place Cessna 152. It is N69061, an airplane I've flown several times before and know well for its inoffensive idiosyncrasies. Out on the dewy grass in front of the Sadler hangars, I'm almost finished with my preflighting — checking the airplane inside and out for glitches and potential glitches — when Ed arrives. He is a short, compact middle-aged man, who resembles, it has often been noted, certain fuzzy, unkempt characters in his own drawings. This morning, he is wearing a floppy hat and carrying a large sketch pad. "So this is the plane we're going in," he says, patting the aluminum skin as if it were the flank of a skittish horse. "It looks neat — small."

I tell him reassuringly that everything checks out fine and the weather couldn't be better. I have found in my limited passenger-carrying experience that involving the passenger in the chores of flying helps to take his mind—and mine—off fantasies of disaster. This scheme works wonderfully with Ed. A briefing on our route, our method of navigation to Stormville, and the simple mysteries of the Cessna 152 put him at ease. He walks through the last stages of the preflighting with me and is interested in every detail. By the time he's buckled into the right-hand seat, he's fairly bubbling with anticipation and asking questions about the sectional chart, with its short penciled line from Danbury to Stormville.

We're all set. I start the engine and call Danbury ground control on frequency 121.60, trying to sound as pro as possible to impress my audience — and, perhaps, myself. We are informed about the wind's direction, its velocity, and the proper altimeter setting, and we are told to proceed to Runway 08.

"Zero-six-one," I respond coolly, with the last three digits of our identification number by way of confirmation, and we taxi to the end of Runway 08 for the engine run-up and final checks. I have not filed a flight plan with the air controllers because our trip is so short and the weather is so good. We will get to Stormville by old-fashioned pilotage: following a corrected compass heading and observing landmarks along the route. After the run-up, I call the Danbury tower on frequency 119.40 and report that I am ready for takeoff, adding that I request a left-turn departure from the traffic pattern. We are cleared. After a quick look around for stray airplanes, I line up on the runway and give it the gun. We hurtle down the paved surface and rise into the sunny eastern sky. I can't resist shouting at Ed over the engine's roar, "Are

Landing at Stormville

you sure you know how to work this thing?" He humors me with a forced chuckle. He is staring out the side window at the brilliant foliage and Greater Danbury below. I can tell that he is totally enthralled. Why not? It's simply beautiful up here.

Out of the traffic pattern and climbing to three thousand feet, we pick up our corrected heading of 342 degrees, into the northwest, and shortly our first pilotage checkpoint — the junction of Interstates 84 and 684, whose tortuous intersecting ramps curl unmistakably beneath the left wing. Ed traces our flight path with his finger over the sectional chart. The next checkpoint is railroad tracks running north and south a few miles farther on, then a tiny pond along I-84, and then — before we know it, big as life — the enormous, grim-walled square of the Green Haven Correctional Facility, which abuts in a shallow valley the narrow strip that is Stormville Airport's lone runway. With the gentle, abetting tailwind, we have arrived far too soon for such a lovely flying day, and I'm sorry that we didn't choose a more distant destination.

The art of setting down at a small field like Stormville, with no control tower and surrounded by other small uncontrolled fields, is to divine what traffic pattern and approach to the runway one should take. Many towerless airports have a radio-communication service called "Unicom," which, if anybody down below is manning it, will give the approaching pilot some advisories on the wind direction, the active runway, and the immediate traffic in the area. However, in this part of the Northeast there is almost always considerable clutter on frequency 122.80, the Unicom frequency in common use. When I call in on 122.80, I receive chatter from Waterbury-Oxford (in Connecticut), Sky Acres (north of Stormville), and Wurtsboro (in Sullivan County, New York), but nothing from Stormville. The Stormville windsock hangs limply, indicating no particular wind in the valley. Since the wind aloft is from the east, I reason that the active runway is 06, into the northeast, not the reciprocal direction of 24, toward the southwest. I can see no other local traffic to give me a stouter hint.

Swinging the airplane into a wide circle to avoid the prison (it is not advisable to fly over prisons, for obvious reasons), I enter the downwind leg for 06 at the prescribed pattern altitude of twelve hundred feet. Flaps down and descending on the final approach, everything going smoothly, Ed and I suddenly spot a flimsy ultralight — the flying lawn furniture of aviation, little more than a hang-glider with an engine — buzzing off Runway 24 like an infuriated yellowjacket, heading right at us. "I guess the active runway is Two-four," I say, with an attempt at coolness, and push the throttle in for a go-around, turning left to avoid the prison. We circle, entering the pattern for Runway 24, and set down easily, rolling to a stop at the taxiway leading to the operations building. Then we park the Cessna on a grassy area near the building, shut down the engine, and step out onto the summery turf. Even with the delay of the aborted first-landing approach, it is only eleven-thirty.

For a weekday morning in October there is a fair amount of activity at Stormville. A couple of student pilots are preparing for their lessons, others fuss with their ultralights at a separate building called the Ultralight Aircraft Center, and the usual hangar hounds are just kind of hanging around. Ed and I stroll into the plain white operations building and introduce ourselves to a chunky young fellow behind the counter. He is Reginald D'Ursel, he tells us in a deep European voice. It emerges that he is a Belgian, an exchange aviation student "piling up my hours, like every other pilot." He is currently piling up his hours by working as one of three instructors for the Stormville Flight School; another of the trio, Albert Kruizinga, is a Dutch exchange student. "Albert and I were in the air forces of our different countries but we learned at the same military flight school," D'Ursel says. "Then we came to the U.S. and got our licenses to teach, so we can learn more here. That's how we are in Stormville, New York. Now, I must check out a student, and then, if you like, I will return to show you around. Make yourselves at home."

We make ourselves at home, sipping some fresh hot coffee — a standard commodity in every small-airport operations building — and striking up a conversation with a student pilot, Roy Spangenberger, who is waiting for his instructor to appear for their appointment. Spangenberger says that he started taking lessons at the large, controlled Dutchess County Airport, near Poughkeepsie, but switched to Stormville because it is ten dollars cheaper per lesson and is a lot less complicated. "I have enough to think about at this stage of my flying without worrying about control towers," he says. "Of course, here at Stormville we have that prison over there to avoid. There were once rumors of prison guards shooting at airplanes that flew directly overhead, but that's probably not true. I'm a technician at the Con Edison Indian Point nuclear reactor — I know, you're going to make a joke about why aren't I glowing or something like that — but it's safer working there than flying. Don't get me wrong, though. I love flying and I can hardly wait to solo. I guess you can say I caught the bug." I tell him that I know the disease well.

Before long, D'Ursel returns. Over more coffee, he tells us the Stormville airport is owned by an elderly couple named Peter and Rose O'Brien, who live in a white house behind some nearby trees. "The O'Briens' daughter, Pat Carnahan, she really runs things around here, making the money all kinds of ways. She's in Florida now on some business deal. On weekends in the summer, this place is a three-ring circus, with ultralights, parachute jumpers, gliders, hot-air balloons, light airplanes, and multiengine corporation aircraft — not to mention the flea market, where people drive and fly in from

Inspecting an ultralight

all over to buy and sell just about anything. That's on one weekend in May, June, July, and August. It's a madhouse here. Eleven hundred dealers and thirty-five thousand customers, all on one hundred and fifty-five acres and a thirty-three-hundred-foot landing strip. I will introduce you both to the O'Briens, but first let me show you the place."

The initial stop on our tour is the Ultralight Aircraft Center, a small white barn serving as a hangar for more ultralights than I have ever seen together under one roof. Despite the disdain of most pilots, the ultralights are catching on because of their relatively low purchase and operating costs. D'Ursel says that he gives instruction in ultralight flying, and I ask him how he does it since the ultralights are one-seaters. "There is a lot of instruction on the ground," he says, "and I also take the students up in a Piper J-3 Cub to give them a feel for flying very light aircraft." Ed, who perhaps would like to learn to fly some day, is unconvinced by the ultralights, however. So am I.

In the rear of the hangar is a real airplane, a very real airplane. It is a Republic Seabee, a wide-body amphibian with a "pusher" propeller (the engine and propeller mounted backwards behind the wing), so there is no obstruction in front of the pilot. The nose of the Seabee can open to provide room for a person to cast flies or dive into a lake; consequently, the Seabee is truly a flying boat, which can also function from land. I have a particular affection for the Seabee. It was brought out by Republic after the Second World War, and an early model was more or less a permanent fixture on a Massachusetts lake where I spent my summers as a boy. The fabulous sight of that lumbering monster roaring off the water, leaving a frothy wake and a majestic spray behind, was the almost daily delight of a plane-crazy kid. The Seabee was supposed to take the place of the family boat and the station wagon — a complete recreational vehicle — but it was underpowered for its weight and design, and too many Seabee

Chuck Basset and his Seabee

owners ran out of water, or terra firma, before they could lift the thing into the sky. Some modifications were made to increase the power, but the Seabee, alas, had its day and its production was discontinued. Pity.

This Seabee in the Stormville hangar must be one of the few flyable ones still around, and it is in mint condition — except for the variable-pitch propeller mechanism, which seems to be in a million metallic pieces on the tarpaulin-covered fuselage. The million pieces are being worked over by a smiling gentleman in his sixties. He takes a moment from his mechanical puzzle to introduce himself. He is Charles "Chuck" Basset — "last name spelled like the dog" — and he is a retired Pan Am captain, from Ridgefield, Connecticut, who until recently flew huge jet airliners. D'Ursel says that Basset probably spends more time in this hangar with his Seabee than he spends in Ridgefield. Basset nods in resigned agreement. He senses my childlike awe of the Seabee and says, "It's a honey, isn't it? I've been the proud owner and fixer of this airplane for eighteen years. It's the 1947 model, which got a lot of bad press back then, but I'm attached to the old thing. Know it inside and out. In the summer, I fly it up to a cabin I own on Long Lake, in the Adirondacks. That lake is so long I call it 'Seabee Lake,' because the Seabee needs so much water to take off from. It's just right for my purposes."

As he lovingly describes its idiosyncrasies, he is interrupted by another Pan Am pilot from Connecticut on a busman's holiday — Steve Adrian, who is looking for a jump cable so he can start the dead left engine of his Aero Commander. "Hey," he says to Basset, "want to sell me that Seabee?"

"Sure, for two million dollars," Basset replies.

"I guess I'll stick with my Aero Commander, if I can only get that damn engine started," says Adrian. "Anybody want to come up for a ride, just say so. It's a beautiful day for sightseeing."

D'Ursel thanks him but says we're going over to visit with the O'Briens. We walk to the O'Briens' house via the parked airplanes out on the grass near the runway. "Who can resist flying on a day like today?" says D'Ursel, surveying the sky. "Especially those airline pilots, who get so much time off. It seems they never get tired of flying."

Peter O'Brien, a bouncy Irishman with white hair and rubicund cheeks, welcomes us at the kitchen door like old friends, to the background noise of a swishing dishwasher and a large, loquacious parrot. He and his wife, Rose, usher us into the quieter living room, where they lose no time in bringing up their favorite subject — the Stormville Airport. "Well, to begin at the beginning, "Peter O'Brien says, "this house was here first, some two hundred and sixteen years ago. It was an inn, originally, for cattle drivers from upstate. All around it was just a big hunk of flat land, ideal for letting the cattle and drivers rest. Then, during the First World War, it became

Camp Whitman, a training base for recruits. After that war, there was a racetrack here, and on October 26, 1927, I arrived and I've been here ever since, building up and running my airport. I suppose I hold some sort of American record as the longest continuous owner and operator of an airport at the same location. This place is certainly the oldest airport in these parts and one of the oldest in the country."

I ask him how he happened to get into the aviation game.

"It started back in the midnineteen-twenties," he answers, "when I was a lad of maybe fifteen. I lived in Westchester County then, going to a one-room schoolhouse with thirty other kids. We called the school a 'swamp college' — Westchester was mostly swamp then — and one fine day a First World War Jenny flew right over the schoolhouse. Well, I'd heard about machines called airplanes but I never had seen one that close before. I couldn't think about anything else. The next day, I found out where that Jenny landed, about ten miles away, so I played hooky and went over to see it. I looked the thing over and over, and that was it — I just had to fly it. I took lessons in that Jenny, and before long I was on my own. In those days, you just hired the airplane and went. No licenses, no federal regulations, none of that stuff.

"Now, I didn't have much of an income — I was too damn young to earn anything substantial — but I worked enough at odd jobs to buy myself an old crate and go barnstorming around the country. I performed stunts like loops and spins, which today look pretty tame, and I sold rides. That was a living of sorts back then. Well, in 1927, I heard about this place. I came here and bought it, trying anything to make a buck — repairing airplanes, instructing, running a charter service, building hangars and renting space in them, anything at all. My big break came in 1942, when the government asked me to train the WASPs here. The WASPs were the Women's Airforce Service Pilots, really more of a civilian private group than a government thing. You see, during the war the military wouldn't allow any civilian flying within fifty miles inland of the coastline, and Stormville was just over the fifty-mile boundary, so that worked out pretty good. We had to stay within a five-mile radius of the airport. We trained a pile of those girls, and they were damn good pilots when we finished with them. They'd come here on their own and stay in different houses around the area, paying their own way since the government didn't contribute anything. From all walks of life they came, some from wealth and some who had to work two weeks to pay for just one flying lesson. We gave them as much primary training as we could in Piper Cubs, Taylorcrafts, Aeroncas, whatever, and then we sent them down to Sweetwater, Texas, for their advanced training. They ended up ferrying B-17s, target-towing, test-piloting — everything but combat. One hundred and twenty-five girls we had here at any given time, along with fourteen instructors, some of them women since it was hard to find men during the war. Every now and then, we'll hear from one of the WASP girls — the Ninety-Niners, they call themselves now. They never got proper recognition, although they sued the government, I believe, for back pay. They were terrific."

Rose O'Brien looks wistful at the memory of those days. "That's about the time I came here to work," she says. "Mr. O'Brien and I got married in 1945. There was so much to do here, stitching and doping fabric and what-all. I personally never learned to fly. I liked it, all right, but the instructors would take me up and scare me to death with spins and stalls. I went up with some lulus."

"We called them 'initiation rides,' " her husband interjects, grinning broadly. "That was the thing years ago, to get you in an airplane and scare the living Jesus out of you. We were doing it wrong, of course, trying to show people how thrilling and dangerous it is. Now, it's just the opposite; we give them 'demonstration rides' and let them take the controls to show them how safe it really is."

Rose O'Brien continues, "Over the years, I've done just about everything around here. I think I know more about most airplanes than some mechanics do. But my three rules are to never prop an engine, to never work on an engine, and to never learn to fly, especially from those balmy instructors."

When the WASP training program ended in 1944, Stormville continued to flourish. It's still flourishing, thanks to the enterprise of the O'Briens' daughter, Pat. "Nowadays, we've got corporate jets coming in here, balloons, jumpers, ultralights, the flea market," Peter O'Brien says. "Some weekends it's a regular field of action, I'll tell you. Over the years, I guess I've seen it all, from Jennys to jets. Some big changes, not all for the better. There's plenty of room for improvement in general aviation. The cost, for one thing. But the people, they still love to fly, no matter what. My daughter's a pilot, and her three children will be pilots one day. Her thirteen-year-old girl is about ready to solo already. It's in the blood."

I ask the O'Briens if any of their closest neighbors, the Green Haven prisoners, have dropped by and expressed a desire to fly, as it were. Peter O'Brien laughs. "Well, since 1938, when it opened, there have been lots of breaks from there," he says, "but they never tried to steal an airplane. When they break out, they're running so fast by here they don't stop for nothing. We're safer than somebody five miles down the road because by then they're tired from running. Once, though, a funny thing happened. Some escapees came by this house and, cool as you please, asked to use our telephone to call for a taxi. Walked right in. The taxi came and they drove off. How's that for nerve? They were captured later on."

Ed and I thank D'Ursel and the O'Briens, and we accept their invitation to return on some summer weekend to see

Stormville in its three-ring-circus mode. Then we preflight the Cessna, share an apple that Ed brought along for the ride, and take off for Danbury, making a leisurely sightseeing side trip over iridescent Dutchess County. The return trip and the landing at Danbury are uneventful, which is the way flying should be.

BACK in 1981, when I was a born-again student pilot, I made a cross-country training flight with Dave Smith, my instructor, to a destination with the impressive name of Sullivan County International Airport. This airport, situated in the heart of the Darkest Catskills, was, I had been informed by Dave, something to behold. "Weirdo," was the way he put it, "like something out of 'The Twilight Zone.' Wait till you see it." Sullivan County International, he explained, was built in 1970 to handle an expected new generation of tourists to the Catskills resort areas from all over the United States and Canada — thus the "international" designation. It boasted an asphalt six-thousand-three-hundred-foot runway, capable of receiving all but the heaviest jet airliners, sophisticated navigational devices, ticket counters, baggage-sorting rooms, and even a U.S. Customs Office. The only trouble was nobody showed up to take advantage of the extraordinary conveniences; the new generation of tourists came to the resorts, all right, but they arrived in their personal automobiles and common-carrier buses, as before. The slick, modern air terminal, maintained impeccably over the years, became a rural monument to misguided dreams of glory — in short, a bust, a fiscal flop. Everything Dave told me about the place was true. We were the only pilots who landed on its magnificent runway that November day in 1981. It was like alighting at La Guardia after a neutron-bomb attack had lethally irradiated New York City.

After our Stormville trip, I told Ed about the Sullivan County International phenomenon and suggested that it was a good place to go for our second excursion, but this time in a heavier, more powerful four-place Cessna 172 Skyhawk. "Physically, it's not exactly a small airport," I said, "but in terms of traffic they don't come much smaller." Ed was interested, and we made plans to fly there.

Wednesday, November 30, 1983
IT is almost two years to the day since I was last at Sullivan County International Airport. Today, the weather is cooperative — cold and clear — and Ed and I once again meet at Danbury's Sadler Aero Center in the morning. One meteorological factor bothers me, however: the wind is coming gustily out of the west. When I file my flight plan by telephone with the Poughkeepsie Flight Service Station, the man on duty there tells me that the winds aloft are as strong as forty-four knots from the direction of 270 at six thousand feet, and the surface wind at Sullivan County International is from 260 at ten knots, with gusts to twenty-five knots. We'll be flying west to Sullivan County at forty-five hundred feet in a sturdy, peppy Skyhawk, N5277E, so the headwind shouldn't be too problematical, but landing on the single long runway could be a headache. That runway is 15–33, and we'll be using the 33 end, heading more into the north than the west; in other words, we'll be experiencing an erratic, blustery crosswind from the left upon landing. When I mention this to my friend Gene Robinson, who operates the Sadler Aero Center, he kids me about having too much runway to put down on in a crosswind. "They got so much runway at Sullivan County," he says, "it'll take you half the day just to taxi up to the tie-down area. It's the perfect place to go if you don't like crowds."

The surface wind at Danbury is straight down Runway 26 at a steady ten knots. No trouble at all. We take off easily, after activating the flight plan with the Danbury tower, and climb to forty-five hundred feet. Ed says he likes the Skyhawk, especially for its roominess and stability as compared to the Cessna 152. I had briefed him earlier on the wonders of avionic navigation — the Very High Frequency Omnidirectional Range stations, or VORs — which we'll be using as a check against our pilotage and dead reckoning, and he is fascinated by the electronic magic of it all. Our first big checkpoint is the rather conspicuous Hudson River, at Beacon, New York, and soon thereafter looms the outspread former Stewart Air Force Base, now a little-utilized relief airport for the busy metropolitan terminals. I call in to the Stewart tower to alert the controllers that I am passing through their control zone, and we press on toward the Catskills ahead. We're making good time in the 172 despite the headwind, but there's some moderate turbulence at the leeward side of the mountains. The airplane rides it well, which pleases both of us. Some cotton-ball cumulus clouds hang high and unthreatening west of the mountains. The resort hotels, golf courses, racetracks, lakes, and highways stand out like beacons below, despite the weak November sunlight. There are the Concord Hotel, Grossinger's, and what look like a hundred imitators; then, dead ahead, an astonishing landmark even from twenty miles away — the Sullivan County International Airport. Ed whistles when he spots it. "It's just like you described it," he says. "What's it doing there? It should be in New Jersey, or someplace like that."

I call the Sullivan County Unicom on the unusually quiet 122.80, announcing my intention of landing on the active runway, which I presume is 33. Indeed it is, a blasé male voice radios back, adding, "Gusts to twenty-five knots from two-six-zero" — a healthy crosswind, classified as Force 6 on the

Beaufort Wind Scale, just below a moderate gale. Ed understands my concern and concentration. He stares straight ahead as we descend for a long final approach and crab into the wind. Soon, we see the VASI — the Visual Approach Slope Indicator, whose red-and-white high-intensity lights guide a pilot to an ideal glide path for a particular runway. The lights show up to us as red over white, meaning in the aviation mnemonic, "You're all right." The rest of the mnemonic is "White over white, fly all night" and "Red over red, you're dead." I repeat the charming rhyme to Ed, by way of explanation and easing the tension. He is enlightened but not calmed.

As our red-over-white glide path takes us closer to the end of Runway 33, I find that I must crab more acutely to the left in order to hold our ground track, the wind is that strong. The length of the runway — continuing on, it seems, to the end of the earth — is no longer a joke; it is a welcome mat of immense value on this crosswindy day. I am thankful for every inch of it. I persist with the heavy left crab until just before flare-out, and then I straighten out the airplane's nose to co-incide with the runway's centerline, dipping the left wing so we won't be blown over. We touch the asphalt on the left wheel and bounce into the air again, veering right. I add a little power and reduce the landing flaps (the former to gain more control and the latter to reduce lift and put the weight on the wheels, not the wings), but the valiant, hard-pressed Skyhawk still veers right, a few feet off the ground. We are caught in the middle of a vicious gust. I consider giving it the gun and going around again — a wise consideration at a lesser airport — but there is so much runway ahead and to the side, I decide to keep easing the airplane down to the ground with more left aileron and judicious additions and subtractions of power. Just when I am beginning to wish that I am some-where — anywhere — else, we settle unsteadily onto the ex-treme right side of the broad runway, all three wheels more or less on the ground. I taxi the airplane toward the tie-down area near the terminal building. Ed is wheyfaced, and I, at the least, *feel* wheyfaced. "Thank God for big runways at small airports," I say. Ed concurs with a loud exhalation. We are

Crosswind landing

arrived, in one piece. A good landing is one you can walk away from, Dave Smith always said.

Slowly, the effect of the dicey landing wears off, and we begin to absorb the "Twilight Zone" atmosphere of the place. I can't tell which is spookier—our arrival or our destination. After we chock the wheels of the shivering Skyhawk and attach tie-ropes to the wings, we walk bent against the cold wind toward the terminal building. Not a soul stirs on this vast, flat moonscape. The only sounds are the caterwauling gusts and the furious snapping of an American flag on its pole in front of the main building. I make a point of counting the machines of various sorts within my view: sixteen tied-down small airplanes, one of which is ours; two fuel trucks; two cars in a parking lot, probably belonging to airport employees. That's it.

Outside the terminal building, everything is pristine and well-maintained. A burnished metal plaque on an exterior slate wall proclaims that this is indeed Sullivan County International Airport, dedicated on June 27, 1970, and financed by the Federal Aviation Administration and a capital grant from the State of New York, County of Sullivan. It also lists each member of the Sullivan County Board of Supervisors and the Airport Commission, most of whom probably would just as soon not have their names so prominently displayed on this colossal white elephant. A chain-link fence, with an open gate, faces the broad, empty tarmac. A sign on the fence reads "GATE 1 PASSENGERS ONLY," but there are no passengers.

Once inside the building and out of the cold, Ed and I take inventory of what we see, our hushed conversation echoing embarrassingly in the ghostly waiting room. We see more plaques, more signs for nonexistent passengers, baggage-sorting bays, ticket counters, a fine slate floor, padded chairs, a free telephone service to the local resorts, placards and pamphlets for automobile rentals and tourist attractions, photographs and paintings of aviation themes, and, most disheartening, yards of empty coat racks. It is as handsome and complete an airport as any medium-sized city in the land could wish for. One of the ticket counters has been given over to a sign-in desk for visiting pilots. I sign in and make use of a direct-phone line to the Poughkeepsie Flight Service Station in order to close my flight plan. The FSS man asks me if I had experienced any difficulties.

"A bit of a crosswind landing at Sullivan," I answer with insouciance.

"I'm not surprised," he says.

A dogleg off the waiting room provides space for a small restaurant, some video games, cigarette and Coke machines, and lavatories. A sign on the wall reads:

DINING AREA

PILOTS, PASSENGERS, AND DINERS ONLY

NO LOITERING!

Ed and I seat ourselves at the counter — pilot and passenger, both potential diners, but we feel like loiterers. At last, a sign of human life. A wan but pleasant-faced woman, her hair arranged in a bun, appears from the kitchen. She regards us with matronizing amusement, as if we were lost children. "You just fly in?" she asks. "Must've been windy. I can hear it howling. What'll you have?" Ed orders fried eggs and coffee; I order a grilled-cheese-and-bacon sandwich and coffee. She retreats to the kitchen and starts cooking, chef as well as waitress.

The food arrives quickly, and it is good. I ask our waitress if it is always this quiet at Sullivan County International. She sighs, shakes her head, and says, "Never gets busy, even in summer. Some student pilots come on cross-country flights, but if there's haze or too much wind on this side of the mountains, they go into Wurtsboro instead. Some years back, there was Ransom Airlines here, which went all the way out to

California, and also a Canadian airline. But they don't come
here anymore. The baggage rooms haven't been used since
then, I don't think. When they built this airport, they thought
people would fly in from all over, but people prefer to drive
up here. We're too close to the city, I guess. Not much charter
service, either, although some private planes with celebrities
come in from time to time, usually during election campaigns.
We had Walter Mondale, Mayor Koch, Governor Cuomo, and
some corporate jets with bigwigs who speak at conventions
and such at the hotels. There's pictures of them on the bulletin board over on the wall. Some people tried to make the
county close us down because of the expense, but since the
federal government put up so much money for the airport, to
pay them back would cost twice as much as it would to keep
the place open. It's not my full-time job here or I'd go broke.
I do painting, too."

As we finish our food, an elderly man and woman, both
puffing on cigarettes, shuffle in from the main parking-lot entrance. They seem to know the waitress well and are apparently regular customers. They settle themselves at a Formica
table and order coffee. With the waitress, they pass the time.
"Loiterers," I whisper to Ed. We pay for the food (very
reasonable) and amble onward, hoping to find more signs
of human life. A door marked "U.S. CUSTOMS OFFICE" is

locked tight, but adjacent to it is the airport administration office, and the sound of radio static crackles from the room. We knock and enter, introducing ourselves to a broody, mustached man behind the Unicom microphone and surrounded by consoles, meteorological indicators, and maps. He is John Lorino, one of the airport administrators, who is also a weather reporter for the Poughkeepsie FSS. He whiles away the inactive hours by chain-smoking cigarettes and drinking coffee. An outer door opens and Tom Nicoletti, also mustached but younger, appears. He is a maintenance man for the airport.

I ask them how many people are on the staff.

"Normally, there are two of us on duty during the day — one in the office and one on general maintenance," Lorino says. "At night, we have a security guard, who also knows how to use the Unicom. And then there's the woman at the restaurant, but she's private, not county. Of course, we got aircraft mechanics over at the hangar, but they're private, too. This time of year it's dead around here."

"Does it ever get what you'd call busy?" I ask.

"Oh, in the summer we have student pilots and corporate airplanes flying in," Lorino answers, "and last summer we had a commuter service going from Albany to here. That's the Tri State Airlines outfit, which has a ticket counter outside. They're not running now. They also fly scheduled flights from Albany to Newark, New Bedford, Martha's Vineyard, Hartford, and so forth, but not from here anymore. When Canadian charters come down, we alert U.S. Customs and they drive over and give them inspections. Sometimes in the summer, we get a charter flight every week. When we first opened, we used to have regular scheduled flights from Toronto, but there wasn't enough business so they pulled up stakes. Also, general aviation has pretty much fizzled out, and that really hurt us. When Labor Day comes, we pull in the sidewalks. It's a big waste. We're one of the nicest facilities in the state, but we don't get much use. There was once talk of putting in an FAA tower here. They don't talk about that anymore."

A pilot calls in on the Unicom. Lorino checks his gauges and radios back, "Active is Three-three, wind two-eighty at fourteen knots, gusting to twenty-five." The pilot decides to land elsewhere.

Nicoletti says, "We're awful high up so we get our windy days, as you guys know. That pilot will probably go into Wurtsboro, where it's less windy. Hell, it's a damn shame. We could handle everything but a Boeing 747 here. What we really need is gambling in Sullivan County, like in Atlantic City. Then things would be hopping. The state probably missed the boat on that one, though. They'll have gambling in the Poconos before we have it. We're all praying for gambling. It's our last hope."

The twenty-five-knot gusts generously abate for our takeoff.

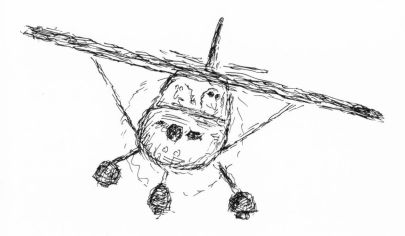

Turbulence

We are in the air and turning toward Danbury before we have covered half the runway. Just east of the Hudson, I let Ed take the yoke of the Skyhawk for a minute. He is like a boy with his first bicycle, joyously encountering the giddy feeling of absolute control. At one point in his excitement, an invisible ripple of turbulence causes the Skyhawk to drop fifty feet or so, and Ed releases the yoke to me as if it were on fire.

"Did I do something wrong?" he asks.

I assure him that he is blameless; it is just aviation's equivalent of the camouflaged pothole in the road. "One of those things," I tell him. "You just learn to ride with it. We'll be home in no time with this tailwind" — and we are, safe and sound.

THERE is something about an island. Whether one travels to an island by water, causeway, or air, the getting there is special, occasionally even more so than the insular goal itself. It's an adventure, it's different, it's fun. For me, piloting an airplane to an island is more fun than traveling any other way. If the weather is good, visual navigation is disarmingly simple. An island just sits out there, its sharp outline ringed by water, rocks, and sand. You have to be a fool to miss it. And flying is efficient and quick — no missed ferries, no crowds, no traffic

Approaching Block Island

jams. As the Cessna Skyhawk flies, it takes about fifty minutes to get from Danbury to, say, Block Island; by car and ferry, it can be the better part of a day.

I knew from past experience that Block Island — officially, the town of New Shoreham, Rhode Island — has a quaint little airport, barely adequate for the summer-tourism demands. In the off-season, however, the airport is a relaxed place. It was for this reason — and because the Block Island State Airport is so different in size and essence from the Sullivan County International Airport — that Ed and I decided to fly to the seven-mile-long isle of greenery and sand, situated halfway between Long Island's Montauk Point and the Rhode Island coastline, before the summer people descended. Throughout the persistently wretched 1983–84 winter that spilled into early spring, we scheduled three flights to Block Island and had to cancel them all at the last minute; bad weather, bad weather, and more bad weather were the reasons. At last, in mid-May, everything was right for the trip.

Friday, May 18, 1984

WE pick another winner of a day. Early this morning, I telephone the Poughkeepsie FSS briefer and he tells me, "It's a perfect VFR day. No precip till after midnight. Block Island reports light and variable surface winds, with at least twenty miles visibility. That's great for Block Island. The wind aloft at three thousand feet is from the north — three-five-zero at eighteen knots." Sounds terrific. I file a flight plan (an especially good idea when aviating over open water) and do my pre-flight calculations. With the moderate wind aloft coming from the north, there should be a slight crosswind as we head east toward Block Island — perhaps more of a tailwind than a crosswind. That will speed up our time en route. The truly good luck is the sparkling visibility and the light surface wind at the Block Island State Airport. That field has a notorious reputation, as the briefer suggested, for troublesome fog or haze and howling surface winds, which are usually at variance to the disturbingly short single runway. Pilots refer to the airport as "the crosswind-landing capital of the world." I had enough crosswind-landing practice to hold me for a while at Sullivan County International.

At eight-thirty when Ed and I meet at the Danbury Airport, we congratulate each other on our good fortune, this perfect day well worth waiting for. Our rented Skyhawk is once again N5277E, a trusted friend to both of us. Her fuel tanks are topped off and she looks eager to fly. We are also eager to fly, but we do a careful pre-flight check, nevertheless. Everything checks out to perfection, complementing the weather. The

Danbury ground controller assigns us Runway 08 (although it hardly makes any difference what runway we use, the surface wind is so light); I activate the flight plan, and off we go. Ed says it's good to be flying again after a five-and-a-half-month hiatus.

We leave the Danbury traffic pattern and pick up a magnetic heading of 101, which compensates for the northerly tailwind-crosswind. Over Bethel, Connecticut, we reach our cruising altitude of three thousand five hundred feet, and Ed, agog at the sunny clarity of the sky above and the world below, has to force himself to perform his cockpit chores. He times our flight between the first two checkpoints — Route 25 and the Housatonic River, a distance of seven nautical miles — and calculates on my Jeppesen CSG-9 nonelectronic flight computer that our ground speed is one hundred and five knots, exactly as predicted. He's getting good at that stuff. We pass over the ensuing checkpoints as planned, and when I radio the Tweed–New Haven tower, the controller says we have clear, nearly trafficless flying through his control zone. Everything is going almost too smoothly. And the aesthetics of this flight on this day are positively breathtaking: the terrain greening in the tardy spring; the Bridgeport–New Haven area thickening into a manufactured marvel; Long Island Sound revealing itself in luminous blue. Over Clinton, Connecticut, halfway to our objective, we can easily make out Fishers Island and, on the horizon, Block Island. Nearer and in sharper focus are the odd hook of land marking the mouth of the Connecticut River at Old Saybrook, the beach at Niantic, and the gray shipyards of New London. The air is like silk. The airplane practically flies itself. We are entranced.

South of Stonington and Fishers Island, we see pleasure boats pushing the season this fine day, and then, all at once, a reminder of the less-placid real world — a fat, black, sinister nuclear submarine, inside the circular wake of its tender. Like so many instruments of war, it has a strange, chilling beauty. We both whistle softly and sigh. But there, over the nose, is Block Island, an unfinished piece of jade set in the shimmering Atlantic.

The nuclear submarine is forgotten, and we start thinking about our approach to the airport. Twenty nautical miles of open sea lie between us and the glistening island, and I am moved to ask Ed, "By the way, can you swim?" Ed is not markedly amused. At ten miles out, just opposite Montauk Point, I radio the Block Island Unicom, giving my identification number and position, and requesting landing information. A friendly, low-pitched voice replies that the traffic is light, the wind is very light, and the active runway is 28. I thank the voice and begin letting down to one thousand feet, so that we will enter the downwind leg at the proper pattern altitude. This means coming in over the ocean, south of the island, turning left to a base leg over the Coast Guard station and the South East lighthouse, and then turning left again for the final approach to Runway 28, announcing my position on each leg. The procedure neatly mirrors the flight — smooth and effortless and inspiring. Ed is already blithely sightseeing, spotting the harbor front and the beaches. The landing itself is as easy and soft as a settling feather. We are down on Shangri-la. It has been an exquisite fifty minutes.

The friendly, low voice on the Unicom tells us to tie down anywhere on the tarmac, there's plenty of room. We park near a few other light airplanes, tie down, and walk to the administration building, enjoying the clean salt air. The building — which looks like a typical Block Island cottage, with its seasoned shingles, white trim, and studied New England primness — is an office, waiting room, and luncheonette combined. A few people are waiting for a scheduled New England Airlines flight to Westerly, on the mainland, while a waitress in the luncheonette sips from a cup of coffee. At the office counter, I close my flight plan by telephone and sign the visiting pilots' register. Inside the office, before a console, sits the owner of the friendly, low voice — a beefy, bespectacled, crew-cut man whose face is as seasoned as the shingles on a Block Island cottage. He is wearing rumpled jeans and a blue shirt. Ed and I introduce ourselves, and the man tells us that he is John Brain, the airport manager. The traffic in and around the airport is still light so we chat with almost no interruptions.

"I've been on the job here for eighteen years," Brain says, "after doing a little bit of everything — except the Army, because they didn't want me. I'm a born-and-bred Rhode Islander and almost a born-and-bred *Block* Islander, since I came here from Providence when I was only two years old. I guess you could say I'm a native, although some people on the island would argue. Besides me, there should be seven other employees for the airport but we're down three — retirements and a termination. The airport is open twenty-four hours a day, seven days a week, and being short-handed right now, we have only one person on every shift. We all do everything around here, no matter what the official position — the Unicom, security, plowing snow, you name it. A new man is starting next week, and hopefully we'll have enough personnel for the busy season coming up."

I ask Brain about the airport's history.

"Well, the state opened the place in 1950," he says. "Before that, there was a big grass field here, and the pilots back then used to land on it informally-like. In 1966, when I started working, the airport was OK for the summer-season traffic, but lately we've been discovered. Nowadays, the runway is too short for the larger airplanes that would like to put in, and we should have another runway for the wind changes. But the state can't get the land now to extend the runway or build another one. They could have once, but now, as I say, we've

John Brain at work

been discovered. Every grain of sand is worth something on
Block Island. If you own land here, it's just a matter of how
bad you want to sell it and how bad someone wants to buy
it.''

Brain is interrupted by a pilot's voice calling in on the Unicom frequency. He wants to know what the active runway and
the wind conditions are. Brain studies his gauges and radios

back that what little surface wind there is comes from the northeast now, so the active is Runway 10 — in other words, the opposite end of 28, which we landed on. "That breeze out there has turned around two or three times already this morning," Brain tells us, "but it's so light it hardly matters. Not many days are this good. We got a certain fame for fog, a wicked crosswind, and that short runway. Some of the hotter airplanes don't make it. I've seen them go over and under the runway, on both ends. Most just about make it. A Cessna Citation jet landed here once, and it just squeaked in. Very little room for error. In case of serious fog, we're still here but the pilots can't find us. They're building a VOR out on the field, but that won't change things too much. We'll still be hard to find in the fog."

Ed wonders aloud how many residents of the island fly in via their own airplanes, and Brain answers that there are thirty-six, almost all of them weekend and summer people. "We got no hangar space available, so they just tie down," he says. "Across the road from the airport, out front there, is a whole mess of beat-up cars. They belong to people who have houses on the island and who fly in one way or another and then use their wrecks to drive from the airport to their houses and back again. After a while, the cars don't start anymore, and so they leave them there to rust. The permanent population is six or seven hundred, but in the summer, well, it's anybody's guess. Thousands and thousands. The ferry boats arrive and two or three thousand people get off. Then the airplanes come in — the private ones, the charters, and the New England Airlines flights — and there are more thousands. The season should begin any good weekend now, maybe this one, although Memorial Day is the usual start of the season. People sometimes come here only for one day. We get a lot of pleasure boats, too, mostly for sport fishing. Some record sport fish are in these waters, like sixty- or seventy-pound sea bass. This used to be the swordfish center of America, but very few are being caught these days. You see advertised on the mainland 'Block Island swordfish,' but they're not really from here."

The talk about fish has given me an ineluctable craving for fried clams, the dish I most associate with Block Island. I ask Brain what restaurant in town he'd recommend. "The choice is very limited," he says. "About the only place open now is Finn's, down by the harbor. Most of the restaurants rely on college kids for help, and the colleges aren't over yet, I guess. Finn's is open all the time, though. You can get a cab out front. It's about a mile and a half into town from here."

We thank him and decide to look around the airport a little more before going into town, my appetite for fried clams notwithstanding. A yellow-and-white Cessna 152 has just landed and is tied down next to our airplane. The pilot and his passenger, both young men, are signing the register at the counter. They tell us that they have flown in from Providence to lunch with a Block Island friend. "A joy ride," says the passenger. "It's such a beautiful day we said, 'What the hell, let's go to Block Island.' " Ed is mightily impressed. "Ah, America," he says to me. "People fly off to Block Island just for lunch. Some life!"

Outside, we explore the airport grounds. The other buildings, a repair hangar and a shed for a fire truck and small bulldozer, are also in the seasoned-shingle saltbox style of architecture. The overall effect is not so much that of an airport as of an unpretentious New England estate. In the hangar, a young mechanic is at work on a green-and-white, six-place Piper Cherokee, while a radio disgorges WNBC rock. The mechanic's name is Rick Jutras, and he works primarily for New England Airlines, maintaining its fleet of airplanes, which include twin-turboprop Britten-Norman Islanders, Cherokee 6's, and a souped-up Cessna Skyhawk.

Jutras takes a break from his work to shoot the breeze — something most mechanics like to do as much as pilots and airport managers. "It's a one-man operation here, with me as the one man," he tells us. "If the job's too big, it's done on the mainland, at Westerly. I'm from Westerly myself. I lived on the island for a year and a half, but now I commute back and forth every day. Since I work for New England Airlines, they commute me for free. I've been stuck out here only a couple of times during the winter, because of the weather. It's beautiful on the island, but in winter it's just plain dull. I always say that this is the airport with the best view in America, especially on a day like today. It's usually about ten degrees cooler than on the mainland, and there's always some wind because there's nothing to stop it, really. You know about our crosswinds. I've seen some doozers here, too. Some pilots come out of their airplanes shaking like leaves. Even *our* pilots, and they know this place better than anyone. It's rougher coming in on Runway Two-eight with that little valley there which makes the wind go nuts. Today's a piece of cake, though. There aren't many days like today."

I ask Jutras if that bulldozer is for plowing snow.

"Hey, Kenny — do we get any snow here?" he yells at a passing maintenance man.

"Snow?" answers Kenny. "What's that? No, we did get about eleven inches in one storm this past winter, but it doesn't really hang around long enough to plow much, which is why we have such a small plow. It's like the Cape — the snow's usually gone by noon. But we make up for it with rain, fog, and wind."

Jutras contemplates his workplace with pride. "You know, what I'd actually like to do," he says, "is get me a sweet little airplane so I could commute back and forth by myself. I'm trying to talk my wife into us buying an Aeronca 7AC that I know is for sale, but she doesn't want to hear about it. This guy I know wants to sell a beauty, with wide-tread tires so you can put it down just about anywhere. It'd be great if I could raise the dough and convince the wife. Some day, some day. Maybe I can get hold of an old wreck and fix it up myself, sort of as a hobby. Maybe."

The prospect of succulent fried clams reasserts itself like a holy vision. Ed and I walk around to the front of the main building to find a cab. The sight of the acre or so of junk cars intrigues Ed, who immediately begins to sketch them from different perspectives. A scarred 1979 Volvo is the latest model present; the others are a mélange of salt-eroded, crumpled Fords, Chevrolets, and Jeeps from the nineteen-fifties and -sixties, parked willy-nilly on the beach grass. A grizzled cab driver, sunglasses glinting under his baseball cap, shouts at us from his vehicle, "Want to buy a car, fellas? Every one of them is for sale, real cheap. It's free parking right now, but there's talk that they're going to be charged thirty dollars a year for the privilege. You won't see many around then, and maybe I can get more cab fares."

We hire the driver to take us into town. "Yeah," he continues as we ride the empty road, "you wouldn't think there were that many people for all those cars, would you? In the winter, though, not much happens. I just take care of my wife. She's an invalid. We people who live here have to work here. Too expensive to commute to the mainland. We make do, though." The taxi passes a vaneless modern windmill by the side of the road. "Our electricity comes from diesel generators, so the government and some private folks thought they'd try these windmills. It's a great spot for windmills but it didn't work out. During our last big storm, the blades flew right off that thing. My light bill is still as high as ever."

Ed and I get off on Water Street, along the harbor front. All around us are the sights and sounds of fixing up for the season — hammering, painting, sawing, window-cleaning. The Hotel

National is displaying a new façade and looks almost antiseptic. We dine alfresco at Finn's, by the ferry slip. As some low cumulus clouds march in from the mainland, I feast on dreamy fried clams, French fries, and a large Coke, while Ed enjoys his fish and chips with a beer. The beer looks particularly good to me, but I have more flying to do today. The other customers are two women in tennis garb and three shirt-sleeved executives on a business trip. The setting is serene and idyllic. Then, at twelve-fifteen, the ferry from Point Judith arrives with a blast of its whistle. Surprisingly, it is jammed with passengers, vehicles, and freight.

"Here they come," says our waitress. "The season has begun." Indeed it has. The passengers are mostly college kids, swarming from the ferry on foot, mopeds, bicycles, and in painted jalopies. Their baggage seems to be limited to scuba gear, surfboards, and guitars. They are, presumably, the summer help, fresh from final exams and ready for anything. The idyllic scene fades along with the sun, which is suddenly blocked by the gathering cumulus clouds. Ed sees me studying the sky and says that maybe we should get back to the airport. I agree.

By the time I file a flight plan at the airport, the cumulus clouds — so fluffy and picturesque a half hour earlier — have merged into a low overcast. The Bridgeport FSS briefer advises that the cloud cover is four thousand feet broken over Block Island Sound and three thousand solid over Danbury. There goes my plan to fly home at four thousand five hundred feet; I'll have to fly at three thousand or less. "The wind's erratic, so it might be a little choppy," adds the briefer. "A front is coming through, about eight hours sooner than predicted." So much for the perfect, glorious day. This is, after all, New England.

Before we depart, we have coffee at the airport luncheonette with John Brain. A hand-lettered sign posted over the

counter reads:"BUY A BUMPER STICKER AND DONATE TO THE SUP-
PORT OF OUR BELEAGUERED ISLANDERS $1.50. FREE THE NEW
SHOREHAM 13." I ask Brain what the local controversy is all
about. He explains that the "New Shoreham 13" are thirteen
town officials who want the power to regulate the noisy and
sometimes dangerous mopeds that invade the island with the
summer tourists. The state authorities have refused to take a
stand on such regulation, and the moped dealers have filed
suit against the locals for harassment. There is even semi-
serious talk of secession from Rhode Island if nothing is done
to control the buzzing bikes. "The natives don't like those
mopeds at all," says Brain, "what with all the noise and the
accidents they cause. We have no hospital here — only a doctor and a rescue squad — so we're forever having to take the
injured from moped accidents to the Westerly hospital. Most
of the ambulance airplanes that put in here are for moped
casualties. It's a real big problem."

We finish our coffee and prepare to leave. The clouds seem
to be getting thicker and lower by the minute. Brain glances
out the window and says, "You should be all right. Nothing
much is supposed to happen till later tonight."

"By the way," I say to Brain, "I forgot to ask if you do any
flying yourself."

"Nope," Brain answers. "In my eighteen years here, I've
flown with others and I know something about it, but I can't
get interested. It's a quick way to go from one place to another,
but as far as doing it myself — nope." Ed looks as if he wants
to question Brain further on this — does Brain know something we don't know? — but I hurriedly bid farewell, and we
head for our airplane on the tarmac. I must guard my passenger's morale.

As promised, the flight to Danbury is fairly low and choppy.
It is also slower than the morning trip, since we're flying
against a variable headwind. And it's far less beautiful. But —

a few lurches and bumps to the contrary — it is uneventful. At four-thirty, an hour after takeoff from Block Island, the Danbury Airport appears below darkening clouds just over the nose. The tower controller gives us permission for a straight-in approach to Runway 26. With all that time to effect a gradual descent to the runway, I manage to perform what is known in the trade as a "greaser" — a landing so gentle that you're not exactly sure when you touch the ground. This pleases me and Ed no end. We are both suddenly weary, but weary with a sense of accomplishment — even if the accomplishment was, essentially, just flying to Block Island for lunch. All in all, it was a lovely day.

FOR our climactic trip, Ed and I agreed that the small airport of destination should be impeccably rural — an authentic diminutive farmer field, a turf strip a long way from anywhere. Since he spends a good deal of time in central Vermont, Ed said that he'd scout the territory for a plausible spot. In short order, he sent me a clipping from the Barre-Montpelier *Times Argus Weekly* about a middle-aged married couple, David and Babs Nutt, who own a tiny farmer field in Post Mills, just across the Connecticut River from New Hampshire. The article indicated that the Nutts were infatuated with their rigorous business and loved flying in all its varieties. The accompanying photograph of the airport and its owners convinced me that Post Mills was ideal for our purposes. I telephoned Babs Nutt and asked if we might meet her and her husband at the Post Mills Airport on Sunday, July 8th, the best date for Ed's and my schedules. I told her that I would fly up to Vermont in a rented Cessna Skyhawk, weather permitting. "That's fine with David and me," she said. "Now, the field is easy to miss in the green countryside, so look for Lake Fairlee to the northeast and a trotting track to the west. The airport is just between them. And watch out for gliders and ultralights when you're landing, especially if it's a pretty good day."

Sunday, July 8, 1984

TODAY is a pretty good day — warm, partly sunny, and less humid after a dismal stretch of heavy rains — and I fully intend to fly the Skyhawk from Danbury to Post Mills, a flight of one hundred and sixty-two nautical miles, about ninety minutes in the air. Since Ed is already ensconced in Vermont, not far from Post Mills, it seems silly for him to travel south to join me for an immediate trip back north again. Instead, we arrange to meet at the Post Mills Airport during the late morning. Just before I am ready to preflight trusty N5277E, I am astonished to learn from Gene Robinson, of the Sadler Aero Center, that his rental airplanes are not insured for solo landings on short turf strips, especially if the fields are soggy from persistent rain. I accept defeat philosophically: maybe it's just as well, what with the cumulus clouds lowering over the northern hills; maybe I am simply not destined to fly this day. One must accept these little setbacks in general aviation. So I get into my car and drive for four hours over broad, steamy Interstates, straight to Post Mills, Vermont. It's no way to arrive at a small airport, however.

The airport, on the fringe of the hamlet of Post Mills, introduces itself by a suspended sign, illustrated with a Grandma Moses–like aerial-view painting of the Vermont countryside:

OPEN ALL YEAR

POST MILLS AIRPORT

EST. DEC. 5, 1945, BY LEN HOYT

RIDES & INSTRUCTIONS

SAIL • PLANE • AEROBATIC

BABS & DAVID NUTT, PROP.

Behind the sign is a surprisingly crowded parking lot, some brown-shingled buildings, a fuel pump, and a few light airplanes and gliders perched beside the grass runways. Since the weather is holding at pretty good, the center of human activity is a redwood picnic table in front of the largest building — really a good-size house. Ed is there, along with some gesturing, gabbing pilots and a blondish, small-featured older man whom I recognize from the newspaper photo as David Nutt. He is wearing sneakers, a brown pullover, khaki pants, sunglasses, and a faded red backless cap with the legend "REGION I SOARING CONTEST" on the visor. To the west, beyond a fence, is the town cemetery, and beyond that is a small ballpark reverberating with the shouts and squeals of a Little League baseball game in full throe. It strikes me that, on a wildly reduced scale, Post Mills Airport is a microcosmic version of La Guardia Airport, which is flanked by the sprawling Queens cemeteries and Shea Stadium.

David Nutt gets up from the picnic table to welcome me. "Babs is down at the other end of the field giving some flight tests to glider pilots," he says. "She's the only federal flight examiner for sailplanes in Vermont, and four people flew up in a Cherokee from Massachusetts this morning for various tests. Let's walk down the strip and watch her, and you can get an idea of what we have here. She's about to take off with one of them in that two-seater Schweizer sailplane." He points to a white blur twenty-three hundred feet away, at the end of the damp runway.

While Ed and I walk with him, David tells us something about himself, his wife, and their airport. A native of Cleveland, Ohio, he is a graduate of Dartmouth (class of 1941) and was a research associate in oceanography at Dartmouth from 1949 to 1981, working much of his tenure with Vilhjalmur Stefansson, the arctic explorer and Dartmouth faculty member, on several frigid expeditions. During the Second World War,

he was sailing about the world for the Office of Naval Research, occasionally returning to Hanover to see his young wife, Babs. In 1966, when the last of their six children was in high school, the Nutts, *père* and *mère*, took up flying with a rare passion. They bought the failing Post Mills Airport in 1979 and have been running it together ever since.

"I was a mariner first, brought up under sail," David says.

"Flying — especially gliding — is for me really three-dimensional sailing. I'm mostly retired now from my professional oceanographic work. I'm so busy with this little airport and an assessing job for the town of Hanover, I can't do it all anymore."

As we stroll along Runway 05–23 toward the parked Schweizer and tow plane, which are joined by a slack umbilical cord of yellow nonstretch polyester marine rope, David points out the other, longer runway, 04–22, and taxi strip. "On good days, we need all the runway space we can get," he says, "because those gliders can't wait to land, and with the ultra-light and power-aircraft traffic it's a little hectic around here. So far today, it's been mostly Babs giving her flight tests. She's in the front seat of that Schweizer, and I think she's about to flight-test one of those Massachusetts people for his certified flight-instructor's rating in gliders."

We stand off to the side and watch a strapping lad, sporting a magnificent curly blond poll, climb into the tow plane and start the engine. The tow plane, David tells us over the rau-cous sputter, is a converted Vietnam vet — a Cessna L-19 "Bird Dog" observation taildragger, kept running by the re-placement of odd parts from here and there. "It's somewhere between being valuable to us as an active tow plane and even more valuable as an antique," he says. "After Vietnam, Amer-ica sold a lot of L-19s and spare parts to Iran, so now it's hard to get what you need to keep them flying. She's a beauty, though, with plenty of power, and we're thankful for that. On a hot day with no wind, it's difficult to pull a glider off the ground without that extra power."

The venerable L-19 taxis out in front of the slightly atilt, sulking glider; the yellow rope tightens, and both aircraft spring to life, churning down Runway 05 into the delicate northerly breeze. Another young man, in blue T-shirt and jeans, runs alongside the glider steadying the wing. The glider is flying before the tow plane is; then both are up and climbing fast. "Babs and her passenger will release the glider at about three thousand feet above the field," David says, "and on a day like today, with few thermals, they'll probably make about a fifteen-minute flight. Normally, the instructor is in the rear tandem seat, but this is a test for a potential instruc-tor, so Babs must act the part of the student, seeing how he works as an instructor. They'll do maneuvers on tow, release procedure, stalls, steep turns, and some slow flight. There's no radio contact with the tow plane or the ground. Don't need it on an uncrowded day. I think there'll be two more glider flight tests of the Massachusetts people — for a commercial license and a private license."

The young man who had steadied the glider's wing now drives up on an orange tractor, and David introduces him to us. He is Mike Eberhardt, who with Phil Gerding, the tow-plane pilot, make up the permanent airport staff — so permanent, in fact, that they both live in an apartment above the office, in the brown-shingled house. Mike is the airport's other glider instructor, and he learned his skills at Post Mills from Babs. A New Hampshire lad early smitten by both power and soaring aviation, he attended Daniel Webster College, an aeronautical school in Nashua, and was directly hired on at Post Mills, where he also performs such chores as tractor-towing the landed gliders to the end of the runway for the next flight.

Above us, the glider has parted company with the L-19; the former is sailing to the west seeking what Mike guesses is a weak thermal, and the latter has peeled off and is making its approach to the runway. The L-19 dips precipitously, releases the yellow rope, which snakes to the ground, and flares out for a smooth touchdown. "He's done *that* maneuver a few times for his years," David says approvingly.

Phil Gerding parks the L-19 and then joins us on the grass strip. As far as David Nutt is concerned, Phil is the *Wunder-kind* of contemporary aviation. Only twenty-one years old, Phil started flying at Schenectady County Airport, near his home in upstate New York, when he was eighteen. "I just went for it and did it," Phil explains. "I've had my flight-instructor's rating since last year. I actually accomplished the whole thing in two years — doing a lot of restaurant work to pay for it all. My family has a camp over at Enfield, New Hampshire, so I did my summer flying at Post Mills. I really like it here, especially since they hired me. Now, I'm working on my commercial glider rating, which means I can take passengers for hire — on sightseeing rides and things like that."

David adds, "Fall-foliage viewing by glider is a major attraction in these parts. It's the only way to see the foliage, according to some people — no noise, no pollution. On certain days in the fall, we have a line of people waiting down here to go up. It's almost a big-time commercial operation." He laughs. "Phil will probably earn his glider-instructor's rating, too, before the summer's over, and then we'll have three glider instructors at Post Mills. We want everybody to be able to do everything."

Babs's Schweizer loses its weak thermal and sinks slowly toward the field, entering the landing pattern. Before long, it whooshes down onto the runway — alarmingly fast, it seems to me. "Gliders go about their fastest when they're landing," Mike explains. The Schweizer brakes sharply and stops dead halfway down the runway, its right wing alop, like a wounded albatross. Mike jumps on the orange tractor and roars off to retrieve the glider for the next flight, while Phil returns to his L-19 tow plane. While the tow-takeoff procedure is repeated for another flight test, David offers to show us around the rest of the airfield.

Besides the two-place Schweizer glider and L-19, the Post Mills fleet consists of a Cessna 152 and a Cessna 172 for sightseeing rides, charters, and flight instruction; a single-place Schweizer for solo soaring; a Bellanca Citabria ("airbatic" spelled backwards) for aerobatic and taildragger instruction; and, the Nutts' pride and joy, a red-and-white 1976 Lake Buccaneer amphibian, which is palaced like a queen in its own special hangar across the runway. "Babs and I go on some long trips with this beauty," David says, caressing the sleek boatlike fuselage. "Last winter, we went to San Diego and Baja California, sharing the flying fifty-fifty. It's a wonderful airplane, but it has some peculiarities. If you're a low-time Cessna driver, you better get a few dozen hours in it before you tackle this one, on land or water. Put the power to it and the nose goes down. If you bleed off power on a downwind leg, the nose tends to go up. You get only about one hundred knots cruising speed because there's a lot of drag, and it's very very noisy and doesn't have much room for luggage or extra passengers, but it's *my* favorite airplane and Babs loves it, too. Once, we flew it to a formal dinner party at a friend's house on Lake Champlain. The trouble was there was no suitable mooring for an amphibian on the shore, so with everybody in their evening clothes watching from the lawn, I stripped down from my evening clothes to my bathing trunks and guided the airplane in toward the beach and secured it. Babs stepped out, dressed to the nines, and then I changed back into my correct attire. It was quite an entrance."

Wandering past an odd assortment of tenant aircraft — including a Piper J-3 Cub, a Schweizer owned by a soaring club, some Eagle ultralights, and an ancient, outsize Cabin Waco in need of heavy restoration — we head back toward the picnic table, where we'll wait for Babs to finish up her flight tests and the attendant paperwork. In the meantime, we chat with Bob Farnham, the redheaded and -bearded third young man of the Post Mills coterie. He has a use-lease on a hangar adjacent to the main house, from which he operates Green Mountain Aerolights — of recent days an exclusive northern New England dealership for the Falcon, which looks like a midget racing car sprouting wings. Bob tells us that the Falcon is the Rolls Royce of its species, with a fuselage made of graphite, Kevlar, and epoxy; a retractable nosewheel; a "canard" forward wing; and even a remote emergency parachute system. "It's the only ultralight for New England flying," he says, with a certain practiced salesmanship. "The Falcon is an extremely stable aircraft, and it has an enclosed cockpit with good instrumentation and controls, and cabin heat for cold-weather flying. During the winter I flew one back from Albuquerque, where they make them, and I never even had to wear gloves. It cruises at about sixty miles per hour, and it just costs about four dollars an hour to fly. This is the only ultralight I'm selling anymore."

I ask him how he got into the ultralight business.

"Well, I came up here in 1975 to go to a small private school nearby," Bob answers, "and I became involved with hang gliders. I thought they were pretty neat, but when I saw a picture in a *National Geographic* of this guy with two chain-saw motors attached to his hang glider, I knew that the extended-flight possibilities were for me. So I took that picture to a friend in North Tunbridge who has a real nice machine shop, and together we figured out how to mount two McCulloch 1010 chain-saw motors, with small propellers, onto my hang glider. We ran off hills with that thing and it was great, until I caught my leg in a prop one day and I realized I wasn't having as much fun as I thought I was. Just a big black-and-blue bruise — no major problem. Anyway, reading some aviation magazines, I saw that others were doing the same thing and calling them 'ultralights.' When I finished school, I went into ultralights commercially, sort of as a small-time venture capitalist. I sold the Eagle ultralights for two and a half years, and now, as I say, I'm into the Falcons only. I can't hardly keep them in stock, they're so terrific. Here, sit yourself in that cockpit and tell me how it feels."

I squeeze into the Falcon's cockpit and, although I'm no ultralight fan, I have to admit it feels good — almost like sitting in a very small airplane.

"If you don't mind waiting a few weeks," Bob says, "I can let you have one for ninety-six hundred dollars, fully assembled and ready to fly." I tell him I'll think about it. Another potential customer pokes his head into the hangar, and Bob goes to work on him.

Ed and I notice that Babs has finally finished up her flight-testing duties and is relaxing with a can of soda at the picnic table. We join her, along with her husband, Phil and Mike, the four visitors from Massachusetts, a couple of other people who just wandered by, and an affectionate brindled airport cat. (As soon as Bob Farnham's potential customer has fully absorbed the Falcon spiel and departed, Bob joins the picnic-table group, too.) It is quickly apparent that Post Mills is not so much a small airfield as it is a setting for an extended family — a family headed by magnetic archetypal parents, Babs and David Nutt. The conversation, the thoughts, the emotions are all directed at or through them. Babs particularly. She is the earth and sky mother. Her trim, youthful figure, her short curly brown hair, her winning smile, and open self-effacing demeanor belie her years. When I manage to monopolize her

attention to ask some questions, conversation halts and every pair of eyes is on her. I ask her about her flying.

"It came to me rather late in life," she says. "I was born Mary Louise Wright, in Englewood, New Jersey — no relation to the Wright brothers, although I'm supposed to be very distantly related to Charles Lindbergh — and I grew up in Scarsdale, New York; graduated from Mt. Holyoke in 1941 — now you can figure out how old I am — and married David in 1943. We came to Hanover permanently in 1946, and I had the full-time jobs of being a faculty wife and a mother. And they *are* full-time jobs. I raised six children in Hanover. Then, in 1966, when the last was in high school, I thought about learning to fly. I had always wanted to fly but I never did it, somehow. Of course, I had been up in airliners, but never in a light airplane. Seeing them overhead tantalized me. So one day I took a flight over the Hanover area with a friend, and I was hooked. It turned out that David wanted to fly, too."

David interjects, "Like Babs, I didn't have time to think about it seriously until after the kids were grown. I started a year or so after Babs. It was lucky we both liked the same thing."

"We began flying right here, at Post Mills," Babs continues. "Len Hoyt was still the owner of Post Mills back then — he comes by to visit from time to time — and a young fellow named Bob Burbank was doing all the instructing. He did a good job on us. I wasn't exactly a natural pilot; it took me about fourteen dual hours before I soloed in the Cherokee we were using then. Learning to fly out of this type of airport is more demanding, and it takes a little more time than average before you solo — but you learn how to fly well. I finally got my private license, in the Cherokee, and about a year later I discovered gliding."

"Around the time Babs discovered gliding," David says, "I was just getting *my* private license. By the way, ask Babs to tell you about her record-altitude glider flight."

"Oh, David," Babs says, reddening a bit. "Anyway, I took my first gliding lesson over at Mt. Washington, but that operation closed down, so eleven of us who loved sailplanes started what we called the Pompanoosuc Soaring Club, named after the river near here. In 1967, we all chipped in to buy a sailplane and flew it out of Post Mills, with Bob Burbank doing the towing for us. And of course I was building up my ratings in power as well as soaring. I received my commercial gliding license from John Schweizer, the son of the sailplane manufacturer, when he was a student at Dartmouth. Now, I'm a certified flight instructor in both power and soaring —"

"And the only federal flight examiner for gliders in Vermont, don't forget," David adds. "My personal best is a private license, with instrument rating, for sea and land aircraft. By the way, do you know that Babs is also an aerobatic pilot?"

I ask Babs about her aerobatics.

"Again, it was just something I was interested in," she answers. "I thought that any competent pilot should have some aerobatic experience — as a way of getting out of tight spots — and in 1974 I saw Jim Holland perform at an air show. He looked like a good teacher, so I took a course in aerobatics with him, using the Citabria here at Post Mills. I found it the most exhilarating thing going. Sometimes I get a little sick but —"

"That's why I never was involved in it," David says. "And I don't have the time to become proficient in it. Besides, I prefer to go someplace when I fly."

"My first aerobatic solo," Babs goes on, "was upriver of here, over an unsettled area. I decided that I'd try a spin first. I must have cleared the area for fifteen minutes before I felt the airspace was free enough of traffic to do a spin. Of course, I had done spins before with an instructor — hanging on to my seat screaming with half-pleasure, half-surprise — but then you have confidence in your instructor's skill. But all alone — that was really something else! Well, I did my solo

David and Babs Nutt

spins successfully, so I went on to the loop. The loop, I love it. That's flying, any day. You do only inside loops in the Citabria; it's not sophisticated enough for an outside loop. But I've flown Cuban Eights, snap rolls, aileron rolls, barrel rolls, and hammerheads in that airplane. You've got to keep up your practice in aerobatics or you lose the touch. To tell you the truth, I haven't done any serious aerobatics in the last two years, and I'm leaving the teaching of it to the younger pilots. You can't dabble in it; either you do it right or not at all. It's really for the young, I guess."

Speaking of the young, I wonder aloud what the Nutts' six children think of their parents' perilous pleasure and business. Were they infected with the flying bug, too? Babs chuckles softly. "They think we're nuts — to repeat an old family pun," she says. "All in all, I believe they were glad to have us out of the house so much. Thank goodness the old witch is busy, they probably said. All six of them became occupied with their own things, none of which involves aviation — kayaking on an international-competition level, sailing, raising families all over the place. They just never found that special something in flying that David and I found. They're indifferent to it, which is all right with us."

THE picnic-table gathering thins out somewhat. The quartet of aviators from Massachusetts announces its imminent departure in the Cherokee, the three candidates for glider ratings having passed Babs's examinations with flying colors, and Bob Farnham leaves to demonstrate his Falcon ultralight to yet another potential customer. The rest of us watch the fully loaded Cherokee taxi to the end of Runway 05. It grinds halfway down the strip in a normal takeoff run, but the pilot realizes that he's not going to lift off the turf in the hot, muggy afternoon air. He aborts the takeoff, slowing for a quick nick-of-time turn short of a ditch before a road and some neighbors' houses at the end of the runway. We are as one transfixed by the sight, and then we all exhale quite audibly. There is that intense concern for every takeoff and landing palpably felt at every small airport I've ever visited. Again, the Cherokee taxis to the end of 05. We hold our collective breath. This time, with more initial up-elevator and flaps, the airplane rises to ground-effect height, gathers airspeed, and climbs easily over the ditch, road, and houses, turning toward Massachusetts. Once more, a collective *"Whew!"*

No sooner has the noise of the Cherokee's engine faded than the grating lawnmower sputter of the Falcon disturbs the peace, as Bob Farnham guns his demonstration ultralight down the same runway. "They're noisy little beasts, aren't they?" Babs says.

"Well, they do exist," David says. "They're a definite part of recreational flying today, and they belong on a small field like this one. You got to roll with the times, I think. If there are too many around here, though, they'll have to find their own farmer field somewhere else or the neighbors will complain."

"Do the neighbors complain a lot?" Ed asks. Especially the ones down at the end of Runway 05?

"So far, no airplane has ever run into that white house at the end of Zero-five," Babs answers, "although just now I had my fingers crossed."

David adds, "The man who used to live there, he said he loved to sit on his porch and watch the airplanes fly over him. All in all, there are five immediate neighbors, and occasionally one of them comes over and complains that he didn't move up here to live next to an airfield. I tell him that the airfield was here before you were."

Babs points toward the cemetery, adjacent to the west boundary of the airport. "Our neighbors on that side are very quiet," she says. "No complaints from them."

"And none of them are ex-students, either," Phil Gerding chimes in.

"In general, though, the townspeople of Post Mills like our being here," Babs says. "They take a certain pride in having an airport in their town, even though not too many of them are customers. The local kids come by on their bikes to hang around, to watch and listen. Some of them save their pennies for lessons. A fourteen-year-old just started to fly gliders. The town crew helps us plow out when the big snowdrifts pile up. It's really tough here in the winter to make a go of it economically, what with the cold, the snow, the fog, the short days, and the cancellations. Once, we thought we'd put the Citabria on skis and rent the airplane out to pilots who'd fly off to the boonies — landing on frozen snow-covered lakes and such — but then we decided maybe it wasn't such a good idea."

"Last winter, we closed down," David says, "and the staff went off to Colorado to ski. We don't know our plans yet for this winter." He goes on to spell out the fiscal problems of owning and operating a small airport. "Flying is a hobby, but running an airport is no hobby," he says. "The whole general-aviation business is slow nowadays. If you're running an operation down in Florida or Arizona, maybe you have a chance to make money on just instruction, charters, repairs, and rentals, but up here we have to drum up business wherever we can find it — a little revenue from this and that to make a living. For instance, we do those sightseeing and foliage-viewing flights in both power and gliders, and we do short daytime charters, photography flights, forest-fire patrols for the state, other forest patrols for lumber companies looking for spreading disease and defoliation, some search-and-rescue work, and we've even been hired to look for lost cows and dogs. Then there are our paying tenants — Bob Farnham with his Green Mountain Aerolights shop, and a combination hangar and house we rent to a mechanic named Skip Kemner — and various tie-down and hangar rentals. We sell maps, manuals, and logbooks in the office, and gasoline out here. We even let parascenders use the field — they're parachute-like gliders towed behind a truck. No skydiving, though. Two years ago, we were the hosts for the New England Region I Soaring Contest, and there were thirty-five gliders on the field and people camping out all over the place. Let's see, what have I left out — oh yes, the banner towing. We make up banners in big red letters for advertising, fairs, birthday greetings, and Phil tows the banner with the Citabria. Yesterday, he flew a banner over Hanover, after the rain stopped. They had a street festival there."

"And as of today, we have a whole new thing going — a banner-towing student," Phil announces. "In fact, here she is." A comely young woman, wearing tight purple jeans and blouse, sandals, and a backward baseball cap, joins the picnic-table group. She is Jennifer Kaufman, a candidate for a commercial-pilot's license. Everyone is quite taken with her, especially Phil, who will be her instructor. "My parents have a summer place in Woodstock," she tells us, "and a regular house in Long Island, but lately I've been living in Southern California. There's a lot of banner-towing work out there, and on Long Island, too, so I thought I'd learn how to do it. Basically, I'm an artist — weaving, tapestry, and millinery design. I hope to make my career in both art and flying." We wish her well in her chosen endeavors, and Phil, all smiles, leads her off to her first lesson in banner towing.

"That's a new one on me," Babs says, shaking her head. "You never know what's coming next in this business. When we bought Post Mills in 1979, we simply wanted it to remain a small airport, with no great vision of a major operation — something for fun and not to lose too much money. Now, it's a labor of love, especially the instruction part. I love teaching, and, I guess, I love teaching gliding most of all. Gliding is my favorite part of aviation, more so now than aerobatics. It's more challenging, since you're dealing with the forces of nature every second. You *use* nature. Each flight is different, different in every place. You never learn all there is to learn."

I figure that this is a good time to bring up Babs's sailplane altitude record. Reluctantly, she agrees to talk about it. She takes me to see the record certificate hanging on her office wall. In the homey office, she is at once diffident and proud. "Well, there it is, the piece of paper that proves it," she says, pointing at the framed document. She elaborates on the official wording: "It was on the fifth of March, 1975, over Black Forest, near Colorado Springs, Colorado. The opportunity came to try for the female two-place altitude record for a sailplane, in a Schweizer 232 all-metal ship. Hannah F. Duncan, of Colorado Springs, was the co-pilot. We released from our tow at about nine thousand feet above mean sea level — Black Forest itself is about six thousand feet above sea level — and we flew for four and a half hours to the record height of thirty-five thousand four hundred and sixty-three feet above sea level. We also won, coincidentally, the female two-place gain-of-altitude record for a sailplane. Luckily, we were in the right place at the right time with the right equipment: oxygen tanks, cold-weather clothing, a sealed barograph to prove our altitude. We flew as gliders usually fly in Colorado — by the mountain-wave effect; that is, by the rising wind on the lee side of huge mountains, not by temperature updrafts from thermals. Actually, you can do that somewhat in Vermont, too. My record for local mountain-wave soaring is twelve thousand feet. But that day in March over Colorado was perfect. Very clear. We just touched a thin cloud layer at the top. No jet traffic. But at that altitude it's a very hostile environment. Stall speed and airspeed are very close together. You balance on a pinpoint, and you have only fifteen seconds of useful consciousness if the oxygen fails. It's about sixty degrees below zero, Fahrenheit, up there. Hannah had electrically heated boots; I wore heavy socks and boots . . . That weird wind noise. That odd light — the startling clarity of light. You are always aware of how small everything is below, how high you are, how beautiful it all is . . . I'd like to do more mountain-wave soaring, but not in search of records. Getting too old, maybe." She looks out the office window at the still sky.

Glider and tow plane

I mention that I have never done any gliding, and after listening to her talk about the sport, I'm eager to try my hand at it. Would she give me my first lesson, perhaps tomorrow? "Well, technically, tomorrow — Monday — is our day off around here," she says, "but I'll be here at ten in the morning if you will. Phil won't mind flying the tow plane for us. He'd rather fly than eat." We agree to meet at the field at ten.

I have dinner nearby with Ed and his wife. The dinner-table talk is, not unexpectedly, about gliding. In this aviatorial case, Ed is the nearest expert; a few years before, he had taken two glider flights at the Warren-Sugarbush Airport, a Vermont soaring competitor for Post Mills. Ed tells me that being in a glider is like imitating a hawk, that it is an otherworldly, unlikely experience. This thought fills my dreams that night.

Monday, July 9, 1984

AT precisely ten o'clock, I am at Post Mills, and so are Babs and Phil. It is their alleged day of rest but they seem as keen to fly as I am. A gentle breeze from the south plays with the maple leaves and some cottony cumulus clouds parade by. Babs says that the "cums" with dark bottoms might signal pretty good thermals, although the ground is still damp from all the rain during the previous week, that dampness tending to cool the air and slow its rising. "You never really know until you try them," she tells me. "In fact, in soaring the more you fly the less you seem to know."

During the pre-flight ritual around the two-place sailplane — N17967, by name — Babs is pleasantly all business. This is a Schweizer 233A, she says, the most common training sailplane in the United States. The Schweizers are built in Elmira, New York. "It's a very forgiving, sturdy bird, although its performance is not terribly high — a twenty-two-to-one glide ratio. My record flight in Colorado was in a Schweizer 232, which is bigger and all metal, with a glide ratio of around thirty-two to one. Of course, that means you can glide thirty-two feet for every foot of altitude." Our 233A has a nose molded of fiber glass; the rest of it is made of both metal and fabric. Like most sailplanes, it has spoilers on the wings — hinged sections that pop up on command to increase drag and thus allow the glider to land at a steep angle, in a kind of controlled crash. Since the flaring-out is slight, a glider landing is rather opposite to a power-airplane landing. The instrument panel and controls are spare: an aneroid altimeter; an airspeed indicator; a variometer for measuring the rate of climb or descent, relative to the horizon; a tow-release knob; a vertical-trim lever; a spoiler-control lever; an air vent; a latch for the plexiglass canopy; and rudder pedals and a control stick. That's all. No compass, no avionics, and, naturally, no engine instruments, which make the aircraft seem ridiculously simple.

But the stark simplicity is deceptive, as I discover when Babs explains how the thing gets off the ground. I am sitting, harnessed and belted, in the front seat, and she tells me from her rear seat about raising the drooping right wing off the turf once we begin to roll, when to apply back pressure on the stick, and how to follow in formation, as it were, with the tow plane. It's a lot to think about on an initial flight, so Babs says that she'll take off and then give me the controls at two hundred feet — the critical altitude for an emergency landing, should something go wrong with the tow. "We take good care of our tow ropes," she adds, "so we've never had any trouble."

With the canopy shut tight, we bake in the hot sun. The tow plane's engine is just a distant whir. Babs wiggles the rudder — the signal to go — and the L-19, Phil's blond mane clearly visible in the cockpit, takes up the tow-rope slack and moves down Runway 23; then a tug, the hiss of the single wheel rolling on wet grass, and we are airborne with amazing rapidity, well before the tow plane. At last, the L-19 climbs out, and with its obedient burden strung behind it, rises over the hills to the south. It is weird and thrilling.

At two hundred feet, Babs says, "This is one of the harder things a student has to learn — following the tow plane in formation. You take the controls and try to hold the tow plane even with the horizon, as you see it." I take the stick with my right hand (I have nothing to do with my left hand, since there's no throttle), rest the soles of my shoes on the rudder pedals, and proceed to make a mess of things. Maintaining a high-tow position, mimicking the tow plane's every movement and holding the proper altitude, is like trying to catch a cricket in tall grass. "Forward pressure," Babs instructs calmly, "now back . . . no, forward again . . . More left rudder . . . more yet . . . Now level out . . . right about there . . . Keep your wings level . . . Oh-oh, you're sinking . . . Keep the tow plane on your horizon. If you drop too low, you'll be in his wake and we'll get some buffeting . . . See? We're buffeting." I realize that I'm overcontrolling — compensating with a heavy hand for my sins, as I did in my early student-pilot days — but this is a whole new ballgame, even more difficult and ticklish. "Make those control movements slight," my instructor warns. Too late. We skid and slip badly. She takes over the stick and rudder pedals, and the glider magically follows in perfect satellite formation with the L-19. "It's sort of a dirty trick giving you the controls on tow the first time out, but you're a licensed pilot and you should pick up the feel quickly." She hands back the controls to me, renewing my shaken confidence, and I find I'm doing a little better.

Out of the Post Mills traffic pattern at seventeen hundred feet, we climb more steeply — six hundred feet per minute, according to the variometer. For the next five minutes, I feel that I'm getting a better sense of coordination. "We're coming up to forty-seven hundred," Babs says, "so we're going to pop off the tow line. This will make a sharp noise when the line releases. Pull the knob when I tell you to. Phil will break left and we'll break right. Keep your eye on him. OK, pull the knob." *Pow!* A party-popper firecracker. The yellow rope snakes toward the accelerating, left-diving tow plane; we turn right, and we're suddenly free, powerlessly alone in the sky — a stupendous sensation, slow and loose and ethereal. The only sound is the soft whoosh of the slipstream, like gentle surf on a sandy beach. We are over the Connecticut River valley, north of Hanover. The Dartmouth campus spreads below, complementing the green hills. Babs trims for level flight and heads toward some cumulus clouds to the west. "We might pick up some rising wind over that ridge," she says. "OK, it's all yours. Hold it at around forty-five miles per hour for the most efficient airspeed. I suggest a coordinated left turn. Use plenty of rudder to compensate for the yaw."

It's tricky, attempting to turn cleanly and not lose airspeed without the help of an engine and propeller, but it's great fun. I hear myself muttering gleeful monosyllables. Before we can pick up more altitude, we fall into what Babs calls a "sink." I balance off the descent with back pressure on the stick, but not so much as to lose airspeed and cause a stall. Babs uses the occasion to describe glider stalls. "This glider stalls very gently," she says. "Just bring the nose up until you feel a slight bubbling and then lower the nose to recover. Try it." I do as she has instructed, and there is a heart-stirring dip, like a silent amusement-park ride. However, the penalty for this instructive amusement is that we have lost a few hundred feet of essential height. "Let's look for a thermal to get back some altitude," Babs says. "That darkish cum over there is a good possibility. If we go a little faster, we'll trade off altitude but cover more ground to get out of this sink and catch that potential thermal. It's a chance you take, trading off one thing for another."

In the crap game of thermal soaring, we lose this particular shoot. The desired thermal under the dark cumulus is nonexistent, probably because of the wet ground. But just ahead is a newly mown hayfield, and once over it, the variometer shows that we are rising at two hundred feet per minute. I can sense the ascent only by watching the instruments; Babs can feel it in her seat. We tightly circle the hayfield, two adults and a substantial machine continuing to rise by sheer force of nature, yet against intuitive natural law. It is extraordinary, unbelievable, even as we accomplish it — not at all a human feeling. The thought occurs to me that we are not so much *imitating* a hawk, as Ed had said the night before, but rather we are *being* a hawk. From the ground, we resemble a giant, stiff bird of prey, but up here we actually are one. Babs tells me that some glider pilots claim to have become friends and fellow travelers with hawks, the birds inviting the pilots to join them in the more productive thermals — sort of like dolphins befriending and helping scuba divers. There is something mystical about all this, almost as if I have departed from my human body and sprouted wings.

But, alas, hawks can flap their wings and continue to fly when they run out of rising air; glider pilots must think about landing at the home airport. The hayfield thermal dissipates and we sink. We have enough altitude to enter the Post Mills pattern at seventeen hundred feet and set up a safe final approach to Runway 23. Babs reminds me that, contrary to power landings, we must increase our speed to about sixty miles per hour and drive the sailplane into the ground, using the spoilers to brake. I follow her coaching, descending to the turf at what seems to me a blistering pace. I flare slightly, apply full spoilers, and touch down with a comfortable jolt.

"Did I do that all by mself?" I ask.

"Yes," Babs says. I am proud and excited beyond measure.

While we retrieve the glider with the tractor and tie it down on its assigned spot alongside the runway, I pepper Babs with a dozen breathless questions. She is indulgent, knowing full well that I'm hooked on gliding. Most of my questions are about extending the duration of soaring. How does one know where to go for the best thermals — assuming hawks don't point the way — and how long can one expect to stay up?

"Well, those cums seemed likely, but they didn't pan out today," she says. "On some days, we could hop from one to another and stay up for hours. I figured on that hayfield as the best spot to gain some altitude. That field usually comes through. We call it our 'house special.' But as I say, you take your chances."

Still a hawk, still floating, I half-walk, half-soar to the picnic table with Babs. The Post Mills agora is untypically empty this day off; David Nutt is in Concord, New Hampshire, on business, and Mike Eberhardt is away on an errand. But before long, a newcomer drops by. He is really an oldcomer — Len Hoyt, who founded Post Mills Airport, in 1945, and is now the seventy-two-year-old grandfather of the Post Mills extended family. Babs and Phil pay him due homage.

"Yep, I come by once in a while," says Hoyt, his hands seemingly sewn into his trouser pockets, his bright-red patterned tam and horn-rimmed glasses accentuating his impishness. "Can't keep away from the old place. But I'm a kept man nowadays. Have a leaky valve, so I don't fly anymore. Go on whale-watching trips off the New England coast, to photograph the big blue whales. Babs and David are old sailors; they know about this."

I ask Hoyt about the pioneer days at Post Mills.

"Yep, well, I was mainly a mechanic back then," he says, "but I also used to fly small airplanes out of the White River Airport, which is now where the post office is. I saw this here field and I said to myself that this is the spot for a farmer airport. After the war, I figured flying was the new million-dollar industry. I ran the airport for thirty-one years. It wasn't any million-dollar industry for me but it was a lot of fun. I did sell Piper Cubs like crazy; a hundred dollars down and a note for twelve hundred more got you a Cub. Hell, that's what a landing gear costs today. We had what we called a dollhouse here at first, with two chairs, a stove, and a fifty-gallon drum of gasoline. Three instructors, at one time. Did a lot of ski operations. Had to break the snow loose from the skis with a pickax handle while the prop was turning, then jump into the airplane. Even had an autogiro here. Noisy little bugger, like them ultralights. But things got too costly. I thought about retiring. Finally sold the place to a man who said he wanted a farmer field and didn't want to make a whole lot of money. I told him he came to the right place. That fellow ran it for a few years and went broke, so he sold the field to the Nutts, who fixed it up real nice with gliders and everything.

"In my lifetime, I met a lot of nice people. Fliers are nice folks — well, I can think of a couple I didn't like so much. The young squirts here kind of upset me sometimes." He motions toward Phil. "Haven't figured this one out yet. He's something else." Phil grins broadly. "Yep," Hoyt goes on, "the last time I flew was in a Cherokee, but I don't think I'll do that again. Maybe, though, if I could just pass that physical . . ."

It's time for me to take to the road back to Connecticut. I dearly wish that I could be flying home. I say my thank-yous and goodbyes, but before I leave I purchase an official glider-pilot logbook from Babs. She endorses the first entry in the book, adding, under Remarks, "Familiarization, tow, turns, thermals." The terse, simple description of my introductory flight fills me with youthful intoxication for my brand-new toy, and I promise to return to little Post Mills to become a hawk again.

Afterword

I could hardly wait to keep my promise to return to Post Mills. At the end of July, my wife, Jane, and I drove up to Woodstock, Vermont, for a week's vacation. As soon as we settled in, I was haunting the nearby Post Mills Airport again, irrevocably drawn by its charming magnet.

During that week, Babs Nutt was out West visiting one of her daughters, but Mike Eberhardt was able and willing to give me my second soaring lesson. In the Schweizer trainer we were towed off by Phil Gerding, released, and immediately accommodated by three generous thermals. We flew tight circles over them for an hour, rising at one point to almost six thousand feet. Another glider joined us in the hottest thermal and, to my utter delight, so did a hawk — the three of us circling and sweeping like heedless, joyful playmates. I was indeed a hawk again. When Mike and I finally had to return to the field — not because we ran out of thermals but because another lesson was scheduled — I felt bereft. I could have been a hawk all day long.

There have been, and will be, other soaring sessions. I hope to earn my private glider-pilot's certificate in the not-too-distant future, and maybe I'll go for an instrument rating in my power flying, so that the weather will be a less crucial factor on long cross-country trips. I have also been toying with the idea of buying into an airplane partnership, certainly a large step up.

For those of us who have caught the aviation bug, there seems to be no cure. The sky is not necessarily the limit. After all, the space shuttle beckons. Hell, if a high-school teacher can go on a shuttle flight, why not a private pilot? So let the rapturous compulsion take its course.

RUNWAY
24
FIRST SOLO
PRIVATE PILOT
OCTOBER
AIRCRAFT FOR SALE
PHONE MESSAGES
READ